D0128375

ACKNOWLEDGEMENTS

Writing a book is hard work, but putting it together in a form for publication — and then publishing it — takes a skill and tenacity that goes far beyond that of the writer. Lucky for me, Connie Gallant, my wonderful wife, best friend, and full partner, has both the needed skill and tenacity for the job. This book would never have been written without her dedication. Her staff at RV Consumer Group has done a marvelous job of keeping the inventory of photographs flowing from database to database to give me the best picks possible.

Every book takes careful editing. With all the chopping and extensive cutting, editing never seems to end. To RVCG's editor, Sasha Sterling, I give my heartfelt thanks for staying with it.

And, of course, my endless appreciation to Roy Easton, Charlotte Landolt, Mary Malone, and Glenn Sharp who assisted us greatly during RV Consumer Group's forming years.

I hope you enjoy learning from this book.

How to Select, Inspect, and Buy an RV

A COMPLETE GUIDE

JD Gallant

Quilcene, Washington
USA

How to Select, Inspect, and Buy an RV
© 2005 JD Gallant

RV Consumer Group
Box 520 • Quilcene, WA 98376

Gallant, JD
    How to Select, Inspect, and Buy an RV
    1. Buying an RV--Purchasing. 2. Recreational
      Vehicles--Purchasing
    I. Gallant, JD
    II. Title: How to Select, Inspect, and Buy an RV
    ISBN 1-890049-9-0
          Third Edition   2005
          Second Edition 2003
          First Edition   2001

NOTICE

How to Select, Inspect, and Buy an RV

Introduction 7

Section 1 — The Search / Select 9

Chapter 1	How to Choose for Type and Livability	11
Chapter 2	There's an RV for Every Budget	49
Chapter 3	Going to Shows and Factories	77
Chapter 4	Being Safe and Legal	107

Section 2 — The WalkAbout / Inspect 141

Chapter 5	Step 1	Profile	147
Chapter 6	Step 2	Skin	163
Chapter 7	Step 3	Structure	177
Chapter 8	Step 4	Roof	183
Chapter 9	Step 5	Chassis	191
Chapter 10	Step 6	Galley	199
Chapter 11	Step 7	Bathroom	217
Chapter 12	Step 8	Woodwork	229
Chapter 13	Step 9	Lining	239
Chapter 14	Step 10	Fixtures	251

Section 3 — The Buy 265

Chapter 15	Rule 1	Prepare to choose in the correct order	273
Chapter 16	Rule 2	Have 5 test questions ready	283
Chapter 17	Rule 3	Visit at least 5 dealerships	293
Chapter 18	Rule 4	Don't trust the salesperson until he/she earns it	305
Chapter 19	Rule 5	Expect a good presentation of each RV shown	315
Chapter 20	Rule 6	Go for the quality!	323
Chapter 21	Rule 7	Choose two dealerships for new and five for used	331
Chapter 22	Rule 8	Have all your facts on paper	339
Chapter 23	Rule 9	Be prepared to walk away	349
Chapter 24	Rule 10	Prepare for back-end pressure	359

Glossary 375

Contents

The RV arena is chock-full of excitement and adventure. It offers many families and retired persons an opportunity to satisfy their inclinations to get away. This is good for our citizenry. The RV arena, however, is lacking in good, solid information about the reliability and safety aspects of RVing. For this reason I will mention *The RV Ratings Guide CD* and RV Consumer Group often in this volume. The intention is not to advertise, but rather to inform. *The RV Ratings Guide CD* is the only consumer publication available for RVs that details specifics about RV value, reliability, and highway control.

RV Consumer Group is a cause — not a business. It is run like a business because that is the only way to keep the cause alive. The organization could not exist without dedicated employees, minimal facilities, and volunteers. Money for research is always lacking. Money for training is always lacking. Money for promotions is always lacking. Without the funding generated through memberships and publication sales — plus the help of our volunteers — we would have a tough time even producing *The RV Ratings Guide.*

I brag about RV Consumer Group because I am proud of what we've done. It has been a formidable task that few understand or appreciate. That we have saved and continue to save many lives cannot be disputed. Our emphasis on safety may be scoffed at by the industry, but it is taken seriously by thousands of potential and active RVers. Although we have made strides toward changing attitudes in the RV industry, we have a long way to go.

So, please don't be surprised if I push safety in the pages of this book. I believe in the lifestyle, and I believe that you deserve all the information available about better and safer RVs.

Section 1

How to Select

Chapter 1

Choosing for Type
and Livability

Choosing for Type and Livability

You can't avoid making choices.

You must make many decisions before finalizing your RV purchase. The surest way to make good decisions is to follow a sequence of steps and then decide as you go through the process. The first step in the selection process is to choose the right type of RV for you. This is a giant step. It'll be one of the hardest steps you'll ever take because, once you choose, you'll know that changing your mind later will cost you lots of money. It's like buying in the stock market: if you put all your assets into one company and that company doesn't pan out, you've lost a fortune. To avoid this, most advisors in stock market trading will tell you to spread your money around. Buy some of this and some of that. You can't do that with RVs. It's not practical to own one of each just to be sure that you made the right purchase for your needs. You're going to have to buy one RV and be sure that it'll be the right one for at least five years. To do this, you will have to make a choice by thinking clearly as you go through this book and walking smartly as you inspect the various types of RVs.

There are ten types of RVs from which to choose.

You're going to find four types of motor homes (class A, class B, class C, class C+); five types of trailers (trailer coach, fifth wheel, toy hauler or sports utility trailer (SUT), telescoping, fold-down); and slide-in truck camper. Each of these types is

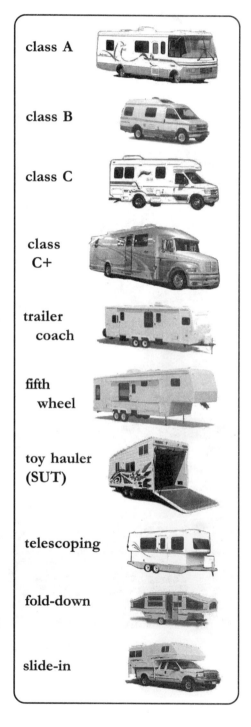

class A

class B

class C

class C+

trailer coach

fifth wheel

toy hauler (SUT)

telescoping

fold-down

slide-in

drastically different from the others. They are structured differently; they have different livability features; and they are much different in respect to highway safety. Just from these three things — structure, livability, and highway control — you can begin to appreciate the importance of choosing according to your personal needs.

Before you select a type, you need to think about size.

Before you consider size, think about where you're going and what you'll be doing when you get there. You also need to think clearly about how long you'll be staying in one place. Once you answer these questions, you'll realize that size is going to be very relevant to your choice of type. The more you focus on size, the more chance there is that your choice of type will change.

As shown in the photos on this page, long class A's will seriously limit your parking options. The luxurious 40-foot pusher with a dinghy had to use the entire parking lot of our small Quilcene post office. While looking for some examples of parking problems in a nearby campground, I came across a long motor home going around and around trying to find an easy place to park. Finally, they just parked in a field. The photo on the

right shows a camping spot that would be paradise for RVs with a total length of no more than 28 feet.

Because most RVs are from 20 to 40 feet long, you will have a considerable range of choices. A 20-foot motor home or trailer is longer than the family car, but it will allow you to get into some of those tight parking places. A 30-foot RV will generally get you into most campgrounds with ease, but they are a bit long for many tourist attractions. Large RVs, especially class A's and fifth-wheel trailers in the 35-foot-plus range, have wonderful homelike features that are not available with smaller RVs, but selecting a long RV will call for some serious compromises.

Fort Worden State Park, Port Townsend, WA

All roads are not equal.

In advance of your purchase, you should determine the types of roads you'll be traveling. In Washington State, RVing often means traveling on roads like that shown in the photo to the right. Traveling in city traffic with a long class A isn't too bad if the streets are straight and you don't have many turns. But a 40-footer on crowded streets where you're turning and passing can be a nightmare. This may be especially bad if your RV is not only long but wide. If it has a long rear overhang, you have to be careful that you don't wipe out an adjacent vehicle or strike a pole. If you have an extra-long wheelbase, you'll need to swing wide for turns and take up most of two lanes of traffic. Professional drivers do this every day, but most of us aren't professional drivers. Our experiences are with 20-foot long cars and trucks. It took

us years to learn to drive these small vehicles, and it's going to take a while to get good at driving a big rig.

And, what about finding a place to park a big rig?

About 50% of private camping sites and about 35% of public camping sites are available for these longer RVs. This means you might have to plan on getting in early and, more often than not, make reservations. If you need a longer RV because it's going to be your home for years, making the compromise is easy. But if you're going for a longer RV to primarily use for weekends and vacations, you may need to reevaluate your priorities.

The upper photo shows a large class A used as a family RV. Because this family apparently enjoys watching TV even when camping, they probably wouldn't venture into the deep woods. You, however, may be different. You may want to get into the wilderness. You need to think and plan this out before you buy.

A small RV will get you into places where you can't take the big rigs.

A small RV can get into the deep woods and crowded tourist attractions where big rigs will do nothing but cause frustration. With a small generator and a few extra containers of water, you can practically disappear into places where most RVers fear to go. Many times you will be able to park a small motor home or trailer in a relative's driveway or backyard without upsetting the neighbors. If you play it right and don't make an issue of live-in activity, you can park just about anywhere for a reasonable period of time. An RV of 15 to 20 feet in length would satisfy more people if they could only get rid of that hang-up of needing a house on wheels. For fulltimers, of course, it's a different story.

The hardest choice will be between a trailer and a motor home.

There are advantages to each. The main differences have to do with what you're going to do with the RV. If you plan on extensive travel, a motor home has some advantages. But on the other side of the picture, many people travel to places where bigger sizes just don't work. Many RVers want to estab-lish a comfortable base camp and then make excursions into the wilderness or to the many tourist attractions available everywhere. You just can't park a 30-foot motor home any place you want to — although an alternative is to tow a small vehicle to get around. The photo to the right shows just that. The couple left their motor home and used their dinghy to visit the local community.

Trailers, especially fifth-wheel trailers, make wonderful homes at a base camp and can allow you some flexibility for excursions with the towing vehicle. But trailer size is relevant because the bigger the trailer, the bigger the tow vehicle. Big trucks aren't the best vehicles for getting into tight wilderness spaces or crowded parking lots. Because compromise will be the big

issue as you take the first step in the selection process, I will cover size in greater detail in chapter 4.

Some people choose motor homes rather than trailers because they're uncomfortable with towing. That's understandable. If you've never towed a trailer, it can be intimidating. Backing can be extremely frustrating for those who just can't get it right. And, don't kid yourself, there are many who can't get it right. I have met some very intelligent and disciplined people who perspire every time they have to back into a camping spot. (Did you see "The Long, Long Trailer" with Lucille Ball and Desi Arnaz?) It's much like playing baseball: There are many who can't hit the ball, no matter how long they practice. So, don't feel bad about not liking to back a trailer — there are other choices.

Class A motor homes tend to excite buyers the most.

I don't know exactly why, but most RVers I talk to are first inclined toward a class A motor home — and the bigger the better. Not all are so inclined, but most will look and consider. It's dangerous to allow emotions to muddle your thought process. You need to stop and think. Maybe even meditate on the subject. "Why," you must ask yourself, "do class A motor homes draw me like a magnet?"

To fathom the reasons for the appeal of class A motor homes would take a baker's dozen of psychiatrists. Just for conjecture, a class A gives a more homelike impression than other motor home types. It's squarish, like a box (and most houses); it has large spacious windows; it has a basement for storage; and the floor plan can easily be designed like a small home. From my conversations with prospective buyers, I found that many like a motor home because they think it drives like the family car — in spite of its larger size. They also like the fact that they have a better view because they're seated higher in the cab. Many buyers, especially men, get a real charge out of the massive number of controls in the class A cockpit, as shown in the photo. It's like an airplane or luxury powerboat. Whatever the reason for its popularity, we know that class A's can make one feel both at home and very important. Those who sell RVs know that emotion sells class A motor homes more than any other factor.

Class B motor homes are more than just small class A's.

Class B's are, in many ways, the opposite of class A's. However, sometimes it's difficult to distinguish between a class A and a class B. Are the two ultramodern-looking motor homes shown on the next page class A's or class B's? Although they look like large class B's, they are, in reality, class A's because they are built on stripped chassis. These *Vixens* were built in the late 80's. Nothing like them has been seen since then. With the new emphasis on fuel efficiency, however, don't be surprised if this style of low-profile motor home becomes

the RV of the future — whether a class A or a class B.

Class B's are perfect runabouts and can be as safe as the family car if well designed. Because the class B is built on a van chassis, RV manufacturers have to be pretty sloppy to mess them up. They do try, however. We have found some class B's that have been so modified and filled with equipment that they are overloaded. Unlike class A's, though, overloading is not common. (Notice that the motor home in the bottom photo looks like a class B, but in reality it is a class C because it is built on a cutaway chassis — as shown at the top of the next page.)

Because class B's are modified vans, we find the cockpit occupants are well protected. Unless the cab has been cut away to install a TV or some other heavy piece of equipment overhead, I believe that the class B can sustain a rollover with as good protection for driver and passenger as any van or truck. Unlike the class A, there is a low-speed collision bumper and a substantial frontal-crush area for higher-speed collisions. There are also safety devices like shoulder harnesses and airbags. For those who are very safety conscious, you can't beat a class B motor home.

You won't find much variety of floor plans, because there isn't much room in a class B. Most class B's have a floor length of about 16 feet and a width of about 6 feet. There isn't much one can do to make more room. Some manufacturers are, however, cutting away some of the side and extending each wall about 6 inches. These are widebody class B's. If done right, a widebody class B can be very comfortable for short-term snowbirds. A small slideout is also available on some class B's. With both widebodies and slideouts, however, you have to be careful about buying one with an overloaded chassis. Notice that the manufacturer of the class B in the photo on this page simply needed to cut a hole in the roof and put a molded cap on the top. This is not the most ultramodern or streamlined motor home design because it appears top-heavy, but it seems to work as long as the suspension is stable.

At one time the class B was a big seller. Sales took a dip as RV manufacturers found out that they could sell higher-priced class A's with lower promotional costs. "We sell every one we can build," the president of a substandard class A motor home manufacturer told me during an interview at an RV show. Sitting next to his big display was a small display of class B's. The substandard class A's were selling in the $120,000 range, and the top-notch class B's were selling in the $80,000 range. There was no comparison in quality — but there was in size. I watched people in their eighties seriously considering a 35-foot substandard class A while the perfect vehicle for them was next door for less money. It didn't make sense to anyone except them.

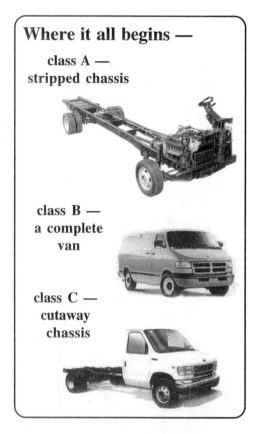

Where it all begins —

class A —
stripped chassis

class B —
a complete
van

class C —
cutaway
chassis

Van conversions

Don't mistake a class B for a van conversion.

A van conversion uses the same chassis and body, but there is generally much less modification and much less equipment. A van conversion is a van converted for comfortable travel – not acceptable for living aboard. You will usually find a van conversion with plush chairs and possibly a place to sleep. Some have room for a porta-potti. Because it does not have a galley (kitchen) or a bathroom, it is not an RV.

As shown on this page, the van conversion, like a van, can be an excellent vehicle for pulling a trailer or just carrying a canoe, if it isn't overloaded in suspension or power. When not in use for RVing, it might work as a utility vehicle.

A class B usually has everything you need.

I said, "need" not "want." Most Americans want much more than a place to eat and sleep. We're used to all that other stuff and, by golly, we're going to have it when we're on the road. So if you need a place to store a washer and dryer, or a sofa to entertain the neighborhood, you don't want a class B motor home. If you need to take it all with you, look someplace else.

Class B motor homes make ideal runabouts.

You cannot beat a class B for getting into and out of campgrounds, tourist congestion, and shopping areas. A typical class B can carry two to four people comfortably almost anyplace you can take the family car. Because class B's range in length from 18 to 22 feet, they are very practical for seniors. Anyone who can drive a small sedan should do okay with a class B.

class B

Of course, the class B is nothing more than a converted van into which some homelike amenities have been installed. These amenities usually include a small galley, a bathroom, and a convertible seating-to-sleeping area. The galley includes a refrigerator that is operated on propane, household electricity (AC), and batteries (DC). Most contain a small television and some may include a generator. As shown in the photos to the right, they can serve as compact homes.

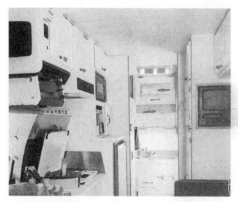

Although the propane container, the fresh water tank, and the waste water tank are relatively small when compared to class A's and fifth wheels, they are usually adequate for trips between campgrounds. Because you don't have holding tanks that supply water or hold waste for a week or more, the class B is not designed to live in as a self-contained home. It is not adequate for boondocking for days on end. You would not have the fuel capacity to keep all electrical appliances and systems operating like you can at home. You would even be hard pressed to find enough storage to keep provisions to last for more than a few days. The class B is a great runabout that can

carry two people and enough supplies for a two- or three-day outing. It's ideal for weekends, vacations, and cross-country

travelers who use campgrounds and maybe an occasional motel. It is also ideal for visiting relatives where accommodations may not be comfortable or convenient. It is ideal for those seniors who like to travel, but are independent enough to want their own space. Those who feel comfortable with these uses should seriously consider a class B. (The photo to the left shows an older class B that serves a tight-budgeted retired couple who still love to camp in the wilderness.)

Consider that a class B will make an excellent long-range traveler for retirement.

Even with the limitations mentioned, a class B can be a compromise for those who would like a class A or class C but

are intimidated by the size, or are at the age when they should be intimidated by size. Having driven big vehicles, I know what I should be driving at my beyond-retirement age. As active and healthy as I am, I am not comfortable driving a big RV in traffic or on high-speed highways. I feel that I would be risking the lives of innocent people if I chose to ignore my newly-acquired limitations. Because I can make a reasonable compromise, it is my moral obligation to do so. Therefore, I choose to either scale down in size or ask someone else to drive.

A class B will let you travel virtually anywhere. I recently spoke with a man in his eighties who was considering taking a

Trip Taylor Bookseller

— HYDE PARK —

Fine used books bought and sold

1607 N. 13th St.

Boise, ID 83702

Phone: (208) 344-3311

Fax: (208) 344-8130

30-foot class A to tour Europe. Just think of all the cost and legal problems involved in shipping, driving license, and insurance. Just think about all those castles, monasteries, and churches with tight parking spaces. You'd have to follow tourist buses to get a parking spot, and then you'd have to worry about being told to move on. If you think our highways and city streets are crowded, wait until you get to Europe! This senior was so far off base that I knew he should not have a class A under any circumstance — in Europe or elsewhere. I hope that I convinced him to choose a class B so that he could travel practically anywhere in the world with relative safety and ease.

When you travel long-range with a class B, make motels part of the budget and schedule. With the money saved by eating in, and with three campground stops for every motel stay, you can justify a bit of luxury. The big bathrooms, the large television, and the giant bed will be refreshing for body and spirit.

As an owner of a good class B, you will find it easy to get into parking spaces and campgrounds. The lack of anxiety of crossing bridges when the wind is blowing, the reduced cost of ferries, toll roads, and toll bridges, and the lack of frustrations normally associated with driving a big rig will make up for the smaller accommodations. If you are a senior, you might even begin to smile a bit more each time you show your Golden-Age pass.

When traveling long-range with a class B, make motels part of the budget and schedule.

The class C is a very versatile motor home.

Because it's built on a cutaway van chassis, the class C, as shown on this page, drives more like a conventional van or small truck. This type of chassis configuration allows the RV builder to design a motor home to the limits of the capacity of the chassis and legal limitations of height and width. The RV manufacturer must leave most of the van's built-in safety features intact to just behind the driver and passenger seats.

Many class C's are designed with a sleeping area over the cab. They have full RVing amenities and are generally available in sizes from 20 to 30 feet. Although some manufacturers build longer class C's, these motor homes are frequently overweight, and I do not consider them safe. Overall safety issues of the class C, including the safety of occupants riding in the house section, will be discussed in chapter 3.

A well-built class C is a good motor home for family use. It can be designed to sleep up to eight, although most are designed for sleeping four to six. The appliances, furniture, and fixtures can be of equal quality to the most expensive class A's. Although the bathroom and sleeping areas may be a bit tight on the shorter lengths, I have found that most are adequate and practical.

Warning! The addition of a cargo bay in the rear to haul your "toys" can be very dangerous. These SURVs (Sports Utility Recreational Vehicles), SUTs (Sports Utility Trailers), or toy haulers with their extremely variable axle weights may create steering and other handling problems.

There are two things that turn off many prospective class C buyers.

First of all, the cockpit does not convert into a living area like the class A. You don't get the open effect toward the front. And then there's that overhead bed. Older RVers don't want to climb into a loft to sleep. Oh yes, you can have a full bed in the back, but that's only with class C's longer than 25' — and that's a corner bed. Did you ever try to make up a corner bed? And when you get a full bed in a 25- to 27-foot class C, the galley and living areas become crowded. "There just isn't enough room," folks tell me all the time. "But of course," the conversation usually continues, "I suppose I could go for a 30-footer with a slideout. That seems to have everything I need." Ah yes, everything you need and an overloaded chassis. As is probably the case with the class C shown on the right. The class C is not for everybody.

Many class C buyers struggle with the value issue.

The scenario is this: Mr. and Mrs. Doe are considering a 30-foot motor home to take the family on weekend excursions and vacations. They like the idea of a class C, but they find that a good class C costs almost as much as a class A of the same length. "The class C has always been for entry-level RVing," they think, "therefore it should be much cheaper than a class A." What they are thinking is basically true. You can buy a cheapo class C for about $10,000 less than a cheapo class A. We should not be interested in cheapo because cheapo is almost certainly a tinderbox and a crackerbox. This means that any cheapo will burn faster than kindling and fall apart in an accident like a sandcastle in a wave. So let's not talk cheapo — let's talk good.

The C+ has everything — for a price.

If the standard class C isn't large enough for you, look at the C+. Unlike the class C (which is generally limited to 28 feet without overweight problems), the class C+ can, and does, provide for motor homes up to 45 feet long while supporting multiple slideout rooms.

Most C+ motor homes are built on commercial truck chassis to give you a good variety of styles and prices. If you think you'll go the C+ way, however, you should plan on spending anywhere between $100,000 and $500,000.

To me, the biggest advantage of a C+ is its crashworthiness. Unlike the class A (which can literally wrap around a tree), a C+ built on a truck chassis is virtually a bulldozer.

For those of you who really want to spend some big bucks to get what your heart desires, a custom C+ is an ideal way to go. There are dozens of small custom manufacturers willing to take your money and your dream plans. But be cautious. It is easy to overbuild on any chassis. Doing so will reduce both the value and the handling characteristics of the vehicle.

Note: Some manufacturers call the class C+ simply a class C, while others call it a Chassis Mount. RVCG's designation of C+ makes it easier to distinguish them from the standard class C which is built on a van chassis.

A step down in size from a class A to a class C can be traumatic.

If your hopes and dreams have been pinned to class A ownership for years, you're going to have to be careful about a quick compromise. Support the compromise with point-to-point reasoning. If you are heavily inclined toward economy or safety — or a combination of both — this should favor a class C. I know of many who have agonized over the subject for months. Many who originally chose a large class A opted for a smaller one with the best in reliability and highway control. Then there are always those few who shrank their expectations all the way to a class B. Most of them decided to do so because they wanted to stay on familiar ground in travel characteristics but were influenced by the safety and economy advantages of the class B. Compromise is good when the thought process is rational.

A travel trailer is always an option.

There are five types of travel trailers: trailer coach, fifth-wheel travel trailer, sports utility trailer, folding trailer, and telescoping trailer. Each one has advantages and limitations. One of the limitations is that you need a vehicle to tow any of them. A big benefit is that the tow vehicle can also be the family car. Almost any family vehicle that has a reasonable engine can tow some sort of trailer. However, trailers longer than 24 feet require a substantial tow vehicle.

The trailer coach is still the number one choice for families.

Families love to load their supplies into a trailer, hook up the family car, and take off for the wilderness or beach. It seems like an ideal way to escape from home. With thousands of models being built every year, you can pick and choose just like you do at the supermarket. Many models in the 28- to 30-foot lengths sleep as many as eight when you include two on the sofa, two in the dinette booth, and two each in the front and rear bedrooms. If the weather turns bad, there's even plenty of room for games, reading, or watching television. And if you want to take a boat along, there are many adaptations for putting one on the roof of the tow vehicle.

The photo to the left shows a European trailer that is common in that part of the world. It is easy to pull and easy to park. For various reasons, I think that in the near future we'll

see more of this style of trailer coach. Just below the European version, you see the American version. We tend to take more with us, so we need a bigger "rig"— which includes a heavy-duty tow vehicle and a much bigger trailer. This configuration has been a popular way to RV for over 30 years.

Trailer coaches have been used by families for recreational homes since the sixties. A good trailer coach almost always costs less than the family car — with which it can be towed. Until fifth wheels got going strong in the late seventies, most snowbirds were pulling trailer coaches south in the fall and north in the spring. There were twice as many trailer coach manufacturers then as there are now, and the overall quality was generally better.

You need a car, van, or truck to tow a trailer coach.

Almost everyone in the U.S. and Canada has at least one

vehicle sitting next to their house that is capable of towing a trailer. Put a hitch on it and off you go. Of course, you do need a certain amount of power, depending on the trailer weight. With weights running from 1,500 pounds to about 10,000 pounds for trailer coaches, you can either choose the trailer to match the tow vehicle, or match the tow vehicle to the trailer.

Either way, it's easy to get it somewhere near right. However, somewhere near right might not be close enough to keep control of the trailer once you hit the highway. Or, it might not be close enough for the vehicle to pull the weight up a long hill without overheating the engine or burning up the transmission.

The tow vehicle must be perfectly hitched to the trailer to make it safe. Never tow a trailer until you understand the various aspects of power, braking, and control of the combination. There are specific rules that must be followed — these are extensively covered in my publication *How to Tow Safely—A Towing Guide CD*. Because these basic rules are violated due to ignorance or negligence, the accident rate for trailer coaches is especially high — even though fatalities are relatively low.

Unlike any other type of RV, just about any floor plan will work in a trailer coach.

Because there are so many RV-related accidents with trailer coaches and smaller towables, I must emphasize that hitching and towing a trailer of any type requires extensive education. If you attempt to tow without skill and knowledge, you will have high risk of a serious accident. (There is more relevant information in chapter 4.)

A trailer coach allows for great latitude in floor plans.

Unlike any other type of RV, just about any floor plan will work in a trailer coach. Because it's like a miniature house, you can have it primarily as a bedroom or galley. You can have the galley in the front, center, or rear. You can have the bedroom in the front, center or rear. You can even have the bath in the front, center, or rear. A common floor plan for families is a master bedroom in the front and bunk beds in the rear. Many seniors love the idea of a big bathroom across the rear with twin beds towards the center. And a big favorite is to place the galley all the way to the front and a walkaround bed

in the rear. Because trailer coaches are usually closer to the ground than class A's, class C's, or fifth wheels, many older people like the single step for easy entry. All these things combined mean you can probably find a trailer coach that will have the perfect floor plan for you.

Trailer coaches generally range in size from 16 to 30 feet. Most are built for weekend or vacation use, but some high-end manufacturers are building them for snowbird or full-time use. (In the photo of the large outdoor family gathering, all the RVs are trailer coaches.) Small manufacturers seemingly do as well, and sometimes better, than the big ones. Competition is keen. There are literally thousands of models of every use classification being produced in varying lengths with every conceivable floor plan. Many are loaded with optional equipment beyond basic needs. All of this, with prices that range from $500 to $1,000 per foot, makes the trailer coach sound so good that it is difficult for the average family not to consider one.

I recommend a trailer coach for certain uses.

A trailer coach is a perfectly good RV for certain uses. It works well for towing behind a sedan, SUV, or van for a visit to the seashore or wilderness. It works well for snowbirds who want to go south in the winter to get away from the snow. It even works well for fulltimers who need to fill the back of their pickup truck with special items. It works well for the professional who needs a place to live when out in the field. It can be very affordable. When purchased new at the right price, depreciation can be minimal. There are literally thousands of used ones available within a short drive from home for most of us. These are all reasons to buy the tens of thousands of trailer coaches being built every year. However, if you can't hitch it right, don't buy one.

For a compromise to big and safe, most RVers go for fifth wheels.

Fifth wheel travel trailers are the most forgiving type of trailer. This is primarily because the design of the fifth wheel puts all the hitch weight on the bed of the truck rather than all the way to the rear. Because an empty pickup is difficult to control under some road conditions, the hitch weight can actually enhance drivability. Of course, you can have too much hitch weight, just as you can have too much load in the bed, but if you do it right, a fifth wheel can be safe and a pleasure to tow.

Because RV size is limited only by law and the size of the truck, most people who want a travel trailer between 30 and 40 feet in length opt for a fifth wheel. With fulltiming almost becoming a national pastime, tens-of-thousands of RVers are using fifth wheels as homes. Many go south in the winter and north in the summer, but there are many who use big fifth wheels as permanent homes. With the average cost of new travel homes ranging from $50,000 to over $100,000, owning a travel home is becoming more attractive — especially when you consider that you can take your home and all your 'stuff' almost anywhere.

Fifth wheel floor plans do not vary as much because the forward area above the hitch is usually the bedroom. This means that the galley is usually in the center or to the rear. A small slideout room is often added in the sleeping area. A 12-foot-long slideout is usually added to the main part of the house to expand the living and dining areas of fifth wheels that are 30 feet and longer. Sometimes, several slideouts are added to give even more room.

The fifth wheel travel trailer makes a good home. With the recent advent of widebodies and slideout rooms, you can get close to 400 square feet of efficient living space. This may not seem like much when many American houses have 4,000 square feet of living space, but seniors or others who use fifth wheels as homes often find them adequate for long-term residences.

The fifth wheel in the photo to the left was designed as an all-weather home. Fifth wheels can have as heavy a chassis and framing structure as the manufacturer deems necessary. They can have large and well-insulated storage basements. They can have a roof adequate to take snow loads in Alaska. They can have a floor, walls, and a roof with enough insulation to keep the occupants comfortable in subzero weather. If it's practical for an RVer to pull, a manufacturer can build it.

There's a fifth wheel for every use.

There are fifth wheels shorter than 20 feet that work well with half-ton pickups, and there are 40-footers that need specially-built midsize trucks. Because most fifth wheels smaller than 35 feet can easily be matched to a pickup truck without any special adaptations, most RVers choose three-quarter-ton and one-ton pickups to pull them. Since both of these pickups can have the same pulling power, the choice comes down to hitch weight.

Half-ton Truck

Contrary to the name, a three-quarter-ton pickup will easily carry a hitch load of about one ton, and a one-ton pickup will carry a hitch weight of about 3,000 pounds, because the hitch configuration moves some of the weight to the front axle. With an optimum hitch weight of 20% of the fifth wheel's total weight, this means that most three-quarter-ton and one-

Midsize (or Medium Duty)

ton pickups can handle fifth wheels that weigh between 10,000 and 14,000 pounds fully loaded. For fulltimers using pickups, this means that pickups with adequate engines can tow most fifth wheels up to 34 feet long. If you are planning on going longer than 34 feet, you should increase your budget to include a midsize truck. (There will be more about the dangers of too heavy fifth wheels in chapter 4.)

A fifth wheel trailer properly hitched to a matched truck will go just about anywhere. In the photo on this page you can see a truck/fifth wheel backing into a wilderness campsite at dusk. They are relatively easy to control going forward or backward.

Toy Haulers can be fun but dangerous.

Call them toy haulers or SUTs (sports utility trailers), these trailers have struck the excitement chord of American families. Just think, you can take all your motorized toys (thus "toy haulers") in their very own well-protected room — it's like adding magic to family outings.

Unfortunately, we are told that these sport-utility trailers are easy to pull and are safe. This is not true. If not properly designed and constructed, toy haulers can be extremely dangerous in three ways: 1) When empty, there could be a heavier-than-normal hitch weight; 2) Loading heavy items in the rear will greatly reduce the hitch weight; 3) A pull-down bunk over "toys" that have fuel and batteries is hazardous to the health and life of sleeping occupants — which often happens when toys are not removed during quick, overnight stops.

Because there is no way to overcome the variable hitch weight when the cargo is loaded behind the axles, you need to compensate with the tow vehicle. Generally, manufacturers move the axles back enough so loading won't lower the hitch weight beyond safety limits, but this is not always the case. Some manufacturers move the axles forward so that the trailer can be towed with a light-duty pickup. This is a problem you need to be aware of.

If you think sleeping in a bunk over gasoline and batteries doesn't make sense, buying a large toy hauler just because you have the power to pull it doesn't make sense. Make the manufacturer and the dealer work for you by providing you with a well-designed trailer that's safe to pull and safe to live in.

A fold-down trailer is a tent on wheels.

Well, not exactly a tent but pretty close to it. They have a hard top, partial hard sides, some regular RV amenities and, in most cases, the rest of it is like a tent. Because the folding trailer is usually well under 3,000 pounds, it is often sold to people who have light tow vehicles. Because many small cars shouldn't pull any trailer, this concept of small pulling small can be misleading. Some people (including salespeople) have the misconception that all that's needed is power. As we're finding out from accidents, you need more than power to pull safely. You also need wheelbase. Without wheelbase there is no stability when traveling.

The biggest problem, other than towing characteristics, is maintenance. A folding trailer is as difficult to care for as a hyperactive teenager. It needs to be treated just right or it'll literally fall apart. It takes special attention to set it up, keep it up, and put it away. You have to be sure it's clean and dry, otherwise it'll begin to smell. If all these things aren't done just right, it's just about impossible to live with. Get the picture?

The fold-down has its place.

A fold-down is ideal for a weekend in the wilderness or at the beach. A fold-down will give you a place to eat, sleep, change clothes, and get out of a surprise rain shower. It's easy to store at home and easy to park at a campground. It's relatively inexpensive.

A fold-down trailer is a wonderful device for vacationing families who want a bit of nature and a lot of economy. With the average new fold-down costing well under $10,000, and used ones selling for under $5,000, there's bound to be something here for every budget. Another good thing about a fold-down is that there's one for almost every family car. Fold-downs can weigh less than 1,000 pounds.

Because of its sensitivity to use and abuse, fold-downs need to have quality to have longevity. Many manufacturers do not consider quality in the equation. They do not consider towing characteristics in the equation. For this reason you'll find about 50% of fold-downs have short lives and terrible towing dispositions. Like a reckless hiker, they are easy to wear out and quick to flip. I'm going to illustrate some good and bad characteristics of fold-downs in chapter 4.

There's a combination hard-wall trailer coach and a fold-down that is called an "expandable" (or "hybrid" because it opens up at the ends for a bed to slide out — much like a fold-down). Although this type is suited for lower-powered, fuel-efficient vehicles, many of these models are,

unfortunately, prone to leak at the front hatch. With good engineering to overcome the deficiencies, however, I think this style of trailer appeals to RVers who prefer to go light and small, but require more space than a fold-down offers.

Actually, there is another type of trailer that is halfway between the fold-down and the telescoping trailer: An A-frame trailer that folds down manually. This is an excellent configuration for couples or small families towing with small vehicles. Like the telescoping trailer, it offers hard-wall security while, like a fold-down and telescoping trailer, it travels with a low profile.

When a trailer coach is too much, there is always the telescoping trailer.

The concept of minimizing air impact while having most of the amenities of a trailer coach is practical. With a telescoping trailer, you simply move the walls up and down as needed. There are only a few added parts, a bit more material, and some good seals. Of course, the interior has to be engineered to allow for cabinets to be below the roof when lowered, but this compromise is minor when compared to the safety aspects of a low profile.

An advantage of a telescoping trailer over a fold-down is its use in the wilderness. Many national parks and forest camps are now forbidding or limiting the use of tents and soft-wall trailers. This is primarily because bears are learning to tear tents and fold-downs to get to the food — and they don't knock at the door. The damages to private property and injuries to campers have increased to such an extent that I would not be surprised if these restrictions are made permanent in some campgrounds.

One of the main reasons for purchasing a telescoping trailer is the ease of towing. There are three characteristics of trailers you need to consider for towing: 1) weight, 2) air resistance,

and 3) placement of the trailer axles. The weight has a lot to do with the amount of power needed and the size of the towing vehicle. The placement of the trailer axle(s) will affect the amount of sway and wobble you'll get when pulling. The amount of impact that air has on the trailer's front and sides has to do with both economy and safety. But keep in mind that a telescoping trailer is quite a bit heavier than a fold-down of the same size. For many owners of small vehicles, a fold-down will be the only choice. I must say at this time, however, that a well-designed telescoping trailer with a non-fixed-ball hitch should be an almost perfect match for many of the SUV's being sold around the world. (There will be more in chapter 4 on this subject.)

Single-axle trailers are here to stay.

With fuel efficient vehicles becoming popular, more RVers are switching to smaller trailers. The easiest way to spot one of these lightweights is to count the axles. If you don't count more than one, you can pretty much figure that the total weight of the trailer will be less than 2,000 pounds. (However, some may go as high as 3,000 pounds loaded.) You will find some single axle trailers weighing less than 1,000 pounds.

First of all, don't let the "single axle" bother you. There has been, and probably still is, a floating myth that single-axle trailers wander a lot. This is bunk. Well-balanced single-axle trailers are super at following the tow vehicle. Unlike tandem or triple-axle trailers, single-axle trailers do not have the resistance to turning that causes the "yawing" (swaying) so common with poorly hitched towing combinations.

Now, where do slide-in campers fit into the picture?

Although the slide-in camper is neither a motor home nor a trailer, it is in some ways a little of each. A slide-in can work somewhat like a motor home because the house is effectively carried on the back of a truck. It actually slides in and out of the bed of a pickup truck. Like a trailer, you must leave the truck and enter the house through its own door. Other than that, a slide-in can be used just as you'd use a motor home.

The slide-in camper has some great advantages. If you own a pickup that you need for utility purposes and you tow a boat for weekend adventures at the lake, you are a prime candidate for a slide-in. A great feature of the slide-in is that, like a trailer, you can unload it from the truck and leave it. If you need a second vehicle and you take occasional vacations but don't do enough RVing to justify a motor home, a slide-in could be attractive. If you find that you don't like trailering but you already have the truck, it might seem practical to try a slide-in camper. If you pull a horse trailer and would like to have housing when you go to horse shows, a slide-in could be just the thing. These are all good reasons to consider a slide-in. The key word here is "consider" — not necessarily "buy."

The major limitation of a slide-in camper is instability.

Although I'll be writing about the safety aspects of slide-in campers in chapter 4, you need to know the number-one reason slide-ins are often traded within a year of purchase. It isn't that they aren't fun or practical, but that most of them don't match the trucks. The proof is concrete. Better than 50% of slide-ins installed on pickups are unstable. Those who use these unstable RVs are always uncomfortable with riding in or driving them. The reasons for this lack of stability are many, but the primary reason is that the buyer listens to the salesperson, who automatically says that going big is okay — and that the proposed truck can carry it.

As you'll learn later, although most salespeople know how to push "buy buttons," they know little about RVing. An excellent buy button is to tell slide-in camper prospects that they can have all the room they need. They talk dry weight but never talk loaded weight or center of mass or center of gravity. They don't mention that the long overhang off the rear will put a "lift" on the front wheels. They don't mention that those high cabinets loaded with supplies will cause rocking and rolling. They don't consider themselves responsible for educating you. The salesperson thinks his primary responsibility is to reinforce your desire to own a big slide-in camper.

Be sure that you choose for livability.

RV Consumer Group has five use classifications designed to help buyers determine how much of an RV they really need. Each classification is based upon the quality of standard equipment. The five classifications are: 1) weekending, 2) vacationing, 3) RV trekking, 4) snowbirding, and 5) fulltiming.

Every brand is assigned a use classification determined by the standard equipment installed at the factory. Each brand must also have a reputation for withstanding the type of activity associated with the classification. A good example of this is the constant downgrading in the quality of the vinyl covering used for the interior. We are seeing vinyl so thin that it can easily wear through within a year of normal use. (See photo on the right.) Another example is that some appliances have been downgraded over the last decade to an extent that many pose a safety hazard when used extensively. You'll see examples of these deficiencies when we do the Walkabout in section 2.

A weekending RV is designed to provide a place to sleep and stay dry.

A weekending RV is not really designed for much more than that. It will not have a complete bath or a complete galley. It might have a porta-potti, a stove top, and an ice box. Although it will always have a place to eat and sleep, it will be as close to camping as you can get without setting up a tent and sleeping on the ground.

Weekending use should not be confused with "cheap." Because weekending RVs are most often used by active families, the interiors should be durable. The basic features and equipment of weekending RVs should keep them inexpensive and light. Most fold-downs, some slide-in truck campers, and a few class B motor homes fit into this category.

An RV designed primarily for vacationing should be well equipped.

Because a vacation RV needs to be adequate for stays up to one month, it will require a full bathroom, but will not re-

quire fiberglass walls for the shower. It will need a basic galley, but will not be required to have heavy-duty venting or an elaborate countertop. Furniture, fixtures, and appliances can be basic. Because vacationers often use their RVs for trips during the cold months, it should have reasonable insulation and good home-environment controls. A class C would be a good example of a vacation-class RV.

You need to consider that a vacation RV is usually marketed to families who generally get away for no more than a few weeks at a time. It may not have to be exceptionally durable, but it must withstand a lot of interior use and abuse so that it will not show wear long before the family has outgrown the RV. When the interior begins to look shabby for any reason, the owners often become less interested in using the RV and more inclined toward selling or trading it. But by this time, it has greatly depreciated because it looks twice as old as it is. Many motor homes and trailers being built and marketed for families are considered substandard by RVCG. These RVs are designed to self-destruct in less than 10 years. Just because an RV is purchased for occasional use, you should never accept lower quality.

For RV trekking you need a tough and well-equipped RV.

If you want to take an RV into the wilderness and stay there for two weeks or two months, you'll need a good RV. Traveling back roads usually means bumps and gravel surfaces. It also means that space size in campgrounds will be limited. You'll also find that services for repairs, fuel, and supplies will be scarce — if they exist at all. Taking an RV into such an environment can be the greatest of experiences — if everything is well planned. This type of activity is called RV trekking.

RV trekking requires that the RV have live-in features and equipment adequate for up to three months' stay. Plus, the entire vehicle must be durable enough to travel country and wilderness roads. For example, RVCG requires that trailer coaches and fifth wheels have shock absorbers or torsion axles as standard equipment for an RV trekking classification. All wheeled RVs need a spare tire. An RV trekking chassis needs to be sturdy and well balanced. The exterior needs to be designed for repelling water. The insulation values should be adequate for temperatures below freezing. The interior needs to have good venting at the windows and through the roof. It needs a durable and practical galley. The bathroom must include good quality fixtures that are solidly fastened. Because RV trekkers tend to be harder on RVs than vacation users, we are adamant that the overall quality be excellent. RV trekking vehicles require many of the features that are characteristic of snowbirding and fulltiming RVs, even though they may not be used for these purposes.

Snowbirding requires an RV that's livable and durable.

When you live in the South during the cold months, you are snowbirding, whether you live in a fixed dwelling or an RV.

This period of time is usually four to six months — or just enough time to get you away from the snow. Snowbirds are usually retired people who feel the cold in their joints or who just want to get away from the snowshovel. Being a snowbird is a great reason to buy an RV.

Arizona and Florida are the two great meccas for snowbirds. They congregate there in RV parks or retirement communities. Whether to live in a fixed dwelling or an RV is often determined by budget or desired lifestyle. If you consider an RV for your housing during your snowbirding experiences, you will probably do so because you want to travel before, during, or after your sojourn. To do so without the frustration of constant breakdowns will require an RV of reasonable quality. As we get into this book, you will learn that many features associated with snowbirding use are standard equipment in RVs that have high ratings for reliability and durability.

Fulltiming can be an enjoyable and rewarding experience with the right RV.

An RV designed for fulltiming is a miniature home on wheels. You cannot

compromise quality if you want good performance. I cannot say that living in a vacation-class RV will always bring disaster to a fulltimer, but it usually brings less satisfaction from the lifestyle — thus shortening its duration. It is sad when an RVing spirit is harnessed to an apartment because the choice of an RV made the experience frustrating. A well-designed and well-equipped RV can bring years of joy to your lifestyle.

Designs

Well-designed
walkaround bed.

Comparable in design to
a small apartment's
bathroom.

Living area designs
are enhanced by
slideouts.

The next photo shows a fulltimers' RV park. Everyone here lives in an RV at least six months each year. Most are using fifth wheels and motor homes longer than 30 feet as their homes. The reason for this is obvious: fulltiming requires more equipment and supplies. You don't have to take everything with you, but you need the essentials. You also need to be able to get around for shopping and visiting. This means you need a "get-around" vehicle. If you pull a trailer, you have the tow vehicle. If you drive a long motor home, you'll need a dinghy. By virtue of their lifestyle, fulltimers don't have to "go home" — because they are at home.

Section 2 of this book will show you that fulltiming requires the best features as standard equipment. Interior features will have to be more homelike to be adequate for fulltiming. You'll want the best of galleys, cabinets, and bathroom features. You'll want excellent appliances and equipment. You'll want superb windows, walls, and ceilings. You'll want the best of workmanship, materials, and design. If you compromise too much, you'll find the cost too high.

There's an RV for
Every Budget

There's an RV
for Every Budget

The purchase price is easy to control.

My brother Bob invested in a race horse. He spent $15,000 for the horse and $4,000 a year on care and fees. If the horse hadn't won a few purses, Bob would literally have lost his shirt. Buying an RV is similar in many ways to horse racing. Your budget has to include both the purchase and the maintenance. There's no chance of winning a purse with an RV, but there's a good chance of losing your shirt.

Many think that buying new is the only way to make a safe RV purchase. Nothing could be further from the truth. Although buying new is usually easier and more predictable, it's predictable because the formulas for cost, loss, and maintenance can be reasonably calculated up front. When buying new, the price you pay for a specific RV will determine depreciation, while the type and brand will be good indicators of future maintenance costs. But when buying new, depreciation losses are always extensive. You can't avoid this. There is no financial incentive for buying new. You must wipe the costs off as the price of enjoyment.

Buying used, however, can cut depreciation losses to a minimum. If you buy right you can actually keep an RV for a few years and show a profit. On the other side of the picture, when you buy new you get a manufacturer's warranty for at least one year. Because prior use history is difficult to verify, the maintenance costs are difficult to control when buying used. In some cases you can soften the effects of costly repairs by buying an extended warranty. But this expensive insurance itself becomes part of the maintenance costs. One thing is for sure: Buying used requires more patience and skill than buying new.

Warning:
"Crackerbox" RVs make up 20% of the RV market.

The beginning of the "crackerbox" era in the 1980's brought too many substandard RVs into the arena. These trailers and motor homes looked good but were destined for fast deterioration because of poor workmanship, cheap materials, and copycat design. It was the natural progression of an unregulated industry that believed in satisfying a price-conscious marketplace. When you are pricing any RV from an appraisal guide, you need to keep in mind that these guides do not consider quality. They are strictly price-oriented, based upon demand at dealerships across the country. Crackerbox RVs are often sold for higher list prices while allowing dealers bigger discounts. The depreciation rates computed into appraisal guides take into account the inflated list prices when new. The risk of buying a crackerbox involves safety as well as economy. Losing a few thousand dollars is bad enough without risking injury or death because of substandard building techniques. To avoid buying a crackerbox, you'll need to study the reliability ratings in the *RV Ratings Guide CD* by RV Consumer Group.

To avoid a crackerbox, you'll need to study the reliability ratings in the RV Ratings Guide.

To get realistic budget numbers, you will need some idea of depreciation, maintenance, and miscellaneous costs.

You will also need to have some idea of how long you're going to keep the RV. I've already mentioned that you need to keep a new one for at least 3 to 5 years. With a used RV, because you'll be buying it right, you can get rid of it anytime you want if it's over 5 years old. If you pay $30,000 for a five-year-old mini motor home, for example — and you keep it for 3 years — you will probably not lose more than 10%, or $3,000, as long as the condition and mileage (4,000 to 6,000 miles a year should be just about right) do not depreciate its value. If you traveled 15,000 miles during the 3 years, your cost-per-mile for depreciation will be 20 cents. Depreciation of $1,000 a year at 20 cents per mile is affordable for most people. All these numbers will be reduced if you buy closer to wholesale.

All purchases should be based on fair-market value.

Most RVs have few maintenance costs during the first five years. Well-built travel trailers should need little repair if treated correctly. Motor homes may need some engine, drive train, or suspension repair, but usually not. After five years, problems will begin to surface — especially on motor homes. After ten years, fixtures and appliances may begin to need special attention. Exterior problems involving roofs, walls, and windows may require some maintenance and repair at about this time. Much of this, however, depends upon the quality of the RV. I have seen two-year-old RVs literally fall apart because the manufacturer had no quality controls and almost no engineering skills. On the other hand, some brands consistently hold up so well that it's difficult to find a single deficiency even after 10 years of use. If you want to figure a cost-per-mile for maintenance, plan on 10 cents per mile for travel trailers and 20 cents per mile for motor homes up to 10 years old.

For motor homes, you will need to figure in your fuel costs at somewhere around 25 cents per mile (year 2005 average), depending on current prices, size of engine, and weight of motor home. If you're pulling a trailer, you'll need to figure about the same for big rigs, and maybe as low as 15 cents per mile for smaller trailers. With trailers you should also figure in the approximate maintenance costs of the towing vehicle.

You have other costs also. You must add your annual costs for insurance, interest (or loss of interest), government fees, and any miscellaneous costs such as storage. These are usually easy to estimate. You probably will want to figure these expenses as annual costs because they are not reduced or increased by highway use. Many RVers figure all costs — including depreciation and maintenance — as annual costs and only fuel as mileage costs. Either way will work, as long as you understand how much you're going to need to go RVing. If you hide your head in the sand, you're going to have financial woes.

> *When you buy new, you will suffer a loss of 25% to 40% as soon as the RV is registered.*

Depreciation of new RVs is quite easy to anticipate.

When you buy new, you will suffer a loss of 25% to 40% as soon as the RV is registered. At that point it is a used vehicle. I know of many individuals who have attempted to sell an RV within a month of purchase and were shocked at the devaluation. In such a scenario, the only hope is to find a "hot" buyer who is willing to save 10% to 20% by buying from a private party rather than a dealer. To most, however, this is not an attractive option because of the lack of choice in colors and floor plan. Of course, dealers won't pay much for an almost-new RV because they buy at wholesale. Sometimes they will buy them back at 20% below wholesale, but that is usually between 30% and 35% off what the owner paid for it. As you can see, you don't want to find yourself in the predicament of needing to sell an almost-new RV.

However, with a good brand, depreciation is about the same at the end of three years as it is during the first year. This, of course, depends on condition. At five years, the average depreciation is about 40% of fair-market value, with a plus or minus of 5% depending on brand, floor plan, and condition. With motor homes, of course, condition includes mileage. With some brands, depreciation is as high as 50% at the five-year mark. After five years, depreciation slows dramatically. Good brands may depreciate as little as 2% a year between the ages of five and ten years. By the time RVs are 20 years old, most depreciate to about 30% of their original cost. At this point, however, much depends on condition. I have found both trailers and motor homes in the 15- to 20-year-old range that sold for 50% of the new price because they were in prime condition — much above the appraisal guide's value listing.

Good brands may depreciate as little as 2% a year...

The average new class A costs between $3 and $4 per mile to own during the first five years.

These numbers are a big shock to many, but they're easy to verify. Just think of this scenario: You buy a $100,000 class A motor home and keep it for five years. During this time, you'll drive it 25,000 miles. Over the five-year period, you spend about $10,000 on insurance and license fees. Your interest paid (or interest loss) will be close to $30,000. Maintenance and mileage will average about 20 cents per mile, or $5,000. Incidental costs will be at least another $1,000 per year, or $5,000.

RVing will not be enjoyable if you are not comfortable with the overall costs.

Now figure in at least $35,000 in depreciation and you'll have a grand total of $85,000 or $3.40 per mile. Because a $100,000 class A is near the bottom of the buying range, the average purchase price is closer to $130,000. And because most RVers keep their motor homes less than five years and suffer even greater depreciation, I think the average cost is realistically closer to $4 per mile. Although $15,000 a year may not be much money for some people `these days, you need to face the facts and know what it's going to cost in the short and long run. RVing will not be enjoyable if you are not comfortable with the overall costs.

Although RVers lose more money on class A's than on any other type of RV, this need not happen to you. If you follow the advice and the rules in this book, you should be able to get into a new RV that will last you 5 years, while keeping depreciation to a minimum. By "minimum" I mean about 35% in the first 5 years of a new motor home's life. An average depreciation from new is 50% for the first 7 years. Between 7 and 10 years you'll be looking at depreciation ranging from 50% to 60%. These numbers are based on average brand, average mileage, and average condition. A better brand, lower mileage, better condition, and better price paid when new can reduce depreciation substantially.

If you trade your class A motor home in two to three years, expect some big losses.

And I mean real "losses." The dealers will make it sound like you won't be losing a penny, but that's just a shell game (as you'll learn later in section 3). Dealers make a lot of money on trades. For the dealer, a good trade is always better than a clean deal. The only way you can keep your losses to a minimum is to buy an RV that you'll keep and use for at least 5 years.

Depreciation begins with the fair-market value of the RV.

All purchases should be based on fair-market value. Fair-market value in RVs is considered to be halfway between wholesale and retail. Retail is based upon manufacturer's suggested retail price (MSRP) for new, and average appraisal book retail price for used. If you pay above fair-market value, you will naturally suffer more depreciation. If you pay below fair-market value, you will suffer less depreciation. Although fair-market value is not always easy to determine, it is also not rocket science.

Paying fair-market value for new is simple.

The first thing you need is a manufacturer's suggested retail price (MSRP) sheet of the specific vehicle under consideration. Because providing MSRP sheets is not required for RVs as it is for autos, you will find that most manufacturers do not provide them. Some manufacturers, however, provide an MSRP sheet or label to the dealers as a guide for retail price. These manufacturers try to control gouging of the public because they know it is bad for their image. The MSRP labels will show the base price of the RV and a list of options that have been installed on the particular vehicle. There will usually be a total that includes the base and the total options price, and then another total that includes the freight. Sometimes, there will be a place where the dealer can add anything he wants for "other services." Added dealer services should be carefully evaluated before including in the grand total. However, the grand total for an RV normally includes only the base price, the total options price, and the freight. This is the number required to compute fair-market price or discount.

> *Although fair-market value is not always easy to determine, it is also not rocket science.*

In the RV industry, dealer cost is about 70% of the manufacturer's suggested retail price. From what I mentioned before, it should be clear that fair-market value will be about 85% of the MSRP. This doesn't mean, of course, that you should pay fair-market value. You should pay as far below the FMV as the dealer will allow. Many RVs are purchased between 75% and 80% of the MSRP. Much will depend on how badly the dealer wants your business or how badly he wants to get rid of a particular RV. (We're going to cover this subject again in section 3.)

If you know actual cash value, you can put pressure on the seller.

Computing fair-market value for used is more complicated.

You must first get the average retail and wholesale prices. The best way to get this is by using *N.A.D.A. Appraisal Guide* and *Kelley Blue Book* values. If you can get both prices, add them together and divide by 2 for an average. Use the paper books (commercial editions are usually found in the public libraries), but if you get them on the Internet, subtract 10%, because that's the amount inflated from the commercial editions to satisfy dealers. Now simply subtract the average wholesale from the average retail, then add half of the results back to the wholesale. You now have a fair-market value for used.

When buying used, however, you should always have some idea of what the actual cash value is. Actual cash value (ACV) is usually about average book wholesale, but it varies from region to region and dealer to dealer. Actual cash value is what a particular dealer will pay, in cash, for a particular unit. Many times actual cash value will be 10% to 20% below book wholesale. For example, in the South during the winter, dealers buy RVs in Florida and Arizona at 20% below wholesale. So, if you know wholesale value, you can put pressure on the seller

— whether a dealer or private party. In this case, private parties are usually easier to work with because they may be anxious to sell to get into that new condo. Of course, if you buy at actual cash value in Florida or Arizona and sell the RV in your home state of Washington, your depreciation could be nil when you sell the RV — especially if you resell at fair-market value.

When you become interested in a particular type, brand, and size, you can easily check prices in classifieds and on dealer lots to determine asking prices. Asking prices usually average about the same as retail. Most dealers and private parties know that most people won't pay the asking price. If you find a dealer "sale" price — and it looks legitimate — you can figure that the dealer will have about 10% to 20% profit in the price. However, never assume that you know what the dealer paid because many dealers know how to buy RVs at far below the actual cash value. Dealers go to auctions, they work estate sales, and they often take in trades at 20% to 30% below actual cash value. Buying and selling used RVs is a great skill that keeps many RV dealers in business. I'll get into the psyche of dealers in section 3.

Of course, a new buyer's loss is a used buyer's gain.

I must say that buying used is the best way for most people to go. North Americans (that includes our good friends in Canada) are generally flexible and practical enough to go used — although many are fearful that a used RV is always a worn-out relic. Nothing can be further from the truth. There are jewels. Except for rubber roofs, slideouts, and the demise of the Dodge and Chevrolet chassis, little has changed in RVs for over 20 years. If you've got a budget above $5,000 for purchase, at least $1,000 a year for maintenance, and reasonable time for a search, you can find an RV that will fit your needs.

Whether your budget is $5,000 or $250,000, you can safely buy used.

You might think, "That's easy for you to say because you know what to buy, what not to buy, and what to pay." It is true that if you lack mechanical and RVing background, it may not be easy. But neither is it difficult if you go slow and are not afraid to ask for advice. (And there's always the *RV Ratings Guide CD*.) You must stick to some strict rules and control your emotions. If you make a mistake, your goal is to be able to correct it without big losses. Keep in mind that 75% of RVs over 10 years old are not going to be acceptable for a variety of reasons. When they're over 20 years old, you'll find that most of them are literally falling apart, with only 25% repairable and 10% in good to excellent condition. This means that you're going to have to spend quite a bit of time on the search. However, you'll be surprised how many RVs you'll find for sale in your community once you start looking.

> *You must stick to some strict rules and control your emotions.*

Used motor homes are more complicated than trailers.

When you buy a motor home, you are buying a truck and a house as one unit. You have to evaluate both segments independently of each other, and then combine them. You begin by checking out the engine, transmission, drive train, and suspension. If that's acceptable, you move into the house. If the house is acceptable, you check out the capacity of the chassis to see if the match is good. If you do these three things in that order, you will be dramatically decreasing the chance of making a horrendous mistake.

When I say, "Check out the engine first," I don't necessarily mean to road test it before you find out if the floor plan works for you. However, if the engine is a 454 Chevrolet in a large class A and has 65,000 miles on the odometer, it will probably be unreliable because it has been overworked. If you're not interested in major repairs and lots of headaches, don't go any further. On the other hand, if it has 15,000 miles on the odometer, give the house a quick once-over to see if it's worth considering. If the house looks like it might work for you, check the gross vehicle weight rating and wheelbase to see if you'll have sufficient payload and acceptable highway control. I'll give you more information on chassis checkout in chapter 4.

Seventy-five percent of RVs over 10 years old are not going to be acceptable.

You might find used class A's built better than new ones.

In the 1980's, many class A's were built with more metal in the sidewalls, and definitely more metal in the front and rear bumper areas. However, the wheelbases were generally inadequate, and the Chevrolet chassis were terrible on just about every motor home over 30 feet long. But there are some models that do work, especially those under 30 feet long. There were also some good diesel pusher motor homes in the late 1980's and early 1990's that were well built — and on good chassis. The search won't be easy, but the savings of tens of thousands of dollars could be worth every moment spent on inspection. And, just think, depreciation could be nil.

Used class A's in the $10,000 range are the most difficult to find.

In 1985, I bought a 31-foot class A for about $10,000. At that time it was six years old with about 50,000 miles on the Dodge engine. It ran well enough to get us moved, with all our belongings, from Southern California to Washington State in three trips. It was in our budget when we bought it, and I sold it in 1988 for $9,600 with about 70,000 miles on the odometer. I put some labor into it, but no money to speak of. Although it was definitely an entry-level motor home, it was a good investment for us because it satisfied our needs at the time.

Finding a class A motor home today for $10,000 usually means finding a worn-out relic, but there have been some jewels. The reason the jewels are available is that the owners don't know the real value, or buyers are afraid of the age. The age of an RV, like mileage, is a good indicator of hidden defects and potential problems. The photo to the left is of a class A of 1970's vintage that could be very usable — and purchased for under $10,000. There is always a risk in buying anything used, but the savings can be substantial enough to dramatically reduce that investment risk — if basic buying rules are followed.

Finding a good 25 -year-old class A can be a challenge.

The biggest problems are the chassis and engine. Dodge dominated the 1970's, and Chevrolet dominated the 1980's.

The Dodge chassis were tough and relatively trouble free, but the engines were finicky, albeit long lasting. Dodge was forced out of the picture by 1980. Chevrolet took over with Ford barely maintaining a toehold on the market. The Chevrolet engines held up quite well to 50,000 miles in the class A's over 32 feet long, and 70,000 miles in shorter ones. The Chevrolet chassis, however, were overload sensitive and generally didn't work well for any class A over 30 feet long.

Finding a motor home with a Ford chassis built in the 1980's or the early 1990's could be the equivalent of finding a jewel. Again, you have to be careful about overloading and short wheelbase. Generally, you can figure that a Ford chassis with a GVWR of 16,000 to 17,000 pounds will work for a class A up to 33 feet long. Anything longer than that and you'd need to see a tag axle attached. With a tag axle — which increases the GVWR by approximately 3,000 pounds —class A's can be as long as 35 feet when standard-built. (However, tag axles often create steering problems on wet and gravelly roads.) With some class A's weighing as much as 18,000 pounds before any people or supplies are loaded, you can see why a long motor home with a GVWR of 15,000 to 17,000 pounds could give you problems with stopping and handling once the RV is fully loaded.

When you buy a motor home, you are buying a truck and a house as one unit.

The big Ford V-8 had a good record for getting a minimum of 70,000 miles before major repairs were needed. With heavy-duty I-beam front suspension, the chassis generally handled well unless the wheelbase was too short. But finding one with reasonable miles on the used market can be really frustrating. Then, when you finally find a good chassis and engine, you might find that the house was built by the wrong manufacturer. As an example: The 1985 Executive motor home shown on the right was well built, loaded with RVing amenities, and sells for well under $20,000. Unfortunately, it has an overloaded chassis. Sometimes it takes a lot of patience to keep going.

Stepping up to a higher percentage of the original cost will get you closer to those cherries.

When figuring depreciation, you calculate from the fair market value (FMV) when new. Forty percent of the original fair market value (OFMV x .40) for example, should get you within 15 years of the build date. For class A's, this will put your buying budget from about $20,000 to $50,000 for gas-driven, and from $50,000 to $150,000 for diesel pushers. It will also increase your chances of finding one in good condition with relatively low mileage. If you work hard at it, it might get you close to the 10-year mark. But, more realistically, you'll be looking at RVs in the 12- to 15-year age range.

If you can go to 50% of the OFMV, you can easily get into the 5- to 10-year age range. There are many RVers who are ready to hang up the towel or trade after 5 years and will take almost any reasonable offer. I've seen many buyers get a practically new RV at 50% of the OFMV. If you find such an RV and change your mind within a few years, you might not even suffer a loss. An example of this is the 8-year-old class A on the left. What a great way to find out if the lifestyle is for you.

Some of the best buys are in the 60% OFMV range.

If you are willing to go to 60%, or even as high as 70% of the fair-market value when new, you'll have practically new RVs at your fingertips. This price range can get you an RV from 2 to 5 years old without a problem. It'll get you the best brands in like-new condition. You'll find what you should be looking for: lots of choices and little future depreciation.

Of course, there are many people who will never buy anything but new. Although I don't have much understanding of this, I can see it if budget isn't a problem. I see a problem, however, when a person buys a new RV and then has to finance it for 15 years. Even when they trade or sell it in 7 years, they'll owe more on it than it's worth. That's not good. Anyone thinking of doing something like this to get into a relaxing and refreshing lifestyle is going at it all wrong. It's so easy and wonderful to buy new when you can afford it; but if you can't afford it, go for used.

Big used class A's are available for any budget.

Big older motor homes are a bargain on the used market. The photos on this page illustrate my point. The top photo shows a snowbird who spends 6 months every year in the Southwestern desert. This vintage motor home is now selling for well under $15,000. The center photo shows a custom-built from a "Skylounge" Greyhound bus generally selling from $50,000 on up. The bottom photo is of a bus conversion that is more conventional, although older than 20 years. These diesel-pusher bus-conversions are usually selling from $50,000 to $100,000. These motor homes may be older, but they usually have lots of life left in them.

You can find entry-level new motor homes (however, most of these are substandard) for not much more than you'd pay for a high-priced luxury car. But if you'd rather buy new, you can go ahead and blow more than most of us will earn in 10 years. Big does not mean better in the RV industry. Because there's much profit in selling big RVs, manufacturers and salespeople push them like glazed donuts. They want you to go big because the profits are big. They don't care if you decide to go smaller within two years (as most do) — they hope you do. Every time you change your mind (as most do), they reap dollars. And dollars

they like. I must warn you that there are many problems with big gas-driven motor homes. These may not be insurmountable, but you'll need to know what they are. (Chapter 4 will cover this subject.)

There are some basically solid small class A's available.

There aren't as many now as there were in the 1970's and 1980's, but you can still find them. It is hard for me to understand why more RVers aren't buying these reasonably-priced and practical motor homes in the 25- to 30-foot range.

Many of these motor homes have lower profiles — which will give them better highway control. They have all the amenities of the larger class A's — although packaged a bit tighter. Because there is a shortage of short class A's, there is a good demand for them on the used market. The photo to the left shows Al and Sunie Weaver, two RVCG members who lived in their 26-foot 1980's motor home for over five years. This is a strong motor home that anyone can find for well under $15,000 with a bit of searching. As long as RV buyers think big is better, however, I'm afraid few manufacturers will venture very far into this smaller market.

Of course, we do have the entry-level diesel pusher market for those who want bigger class A's.

One of the biggest booms in the RV industry began in the mid-1990's when RVCG started questioning the safety of many gas-driven class A's. Those who were safety conscious wanted something better, so they started buying entry-level diesel pushers. As a rule, these were superior in safety and efficiency to the average gas-driven motor home. With prices ranging from $100,000 to $150,000, manufacturers of these class A's found many buyers. A great benefit of these entry-level diesel pushers is the low depreciation because of the demand for used ones. It seems that 50% of motor home buyers prefer a used diesel pusher to a new gas-driven class A. Even though the prices have slowly climbed during the past decade, the entry-level diesel pusher still attracts many RVers who want larger motor homes and have given up on gasoline.

Used diesel pushers are demanding big prices.

Used diesel pushers, like the one shown on the right, are in big demand. This has kept prices inflated on the used market. Since the mid-1990's new sales have increased — primarily because of the influx of entry-level pushers. The law of supply-and-demand and the habits of RVers tell us that we can expect used diesel pushers to become increasingly available after 2005. I think that you'll find a lower depreciation rate for these motor homes in the near future.

There's a big move to quarter-million-dollar-plus motor homes.

Two hundred and fifty thousand dollars is a lot of money for many people, including me. If you're in this buying range, you probably have enough assets that you're not going to worry about little things. However, even though you may have lots of money, you will not be happy about buying an expensive motor home that could give you ulcers. You don't call the mechanic every time you hear a rattle in a custom motor home — as you would with an expensive car. The manufacturer often wants the vehicle back at their factory. If it breaks down, you don't call just any wrecker — you wait for a mechanic and, if needed, you wait for a special wrecker. Because it's a high-tech piece of equipment, be prepared for some problems.

The reputation of a high-end motor home builder is paramount. You need to study its corporate portfolio just as you

would when buying a block of its stock. You need to know the manufacturer's attitude toward the safety and reliability of its brands. Just because a motor home is loaded with a big engine and has lots of glitter doesn't mean it's reliable and safe. Believe me, there are good high-end builders and bad ones. You need to know the difference.

There is **BIG** depreciation in big motor homes such as the one shown on the left. This is especially true of those high-ends that cost between $250,000 and $500,000 new. One of the reasons for this is that there's a good supply of them on the used market. Another reason is that most people who have that much money to spend don't want something used. If you plan on a 40% to 50% depreciation beginning with the first day of ownership, you won't be shocked later. The only reason I know this is that, in the past, I've helped people find almost new ones. And, believe me, it isn't that hard to find one at a bargain price.

Used class B's are in big demand.

It's almost impossible to find a good used class B with low mileage — and I always recommend low mileage for any motor home. Many class B's on the used market, however, have had very little use in the galley and sleeping areas. We have found class B's between 6 and 7 years old with galleys that have hardly been used. The problem is mileage. While the average for class A's is 5,000 miles a year, class B's get close to 10,000. On the other side of the picture, however, a gas-driven class A's engine is overworking all the time, while a class B's engine is rarely overtaxed. This makes the mileage on a class B about equal to half the mileage on a class A. Gas-driven class A engines are usually worn out at 70,000 miles, but class B engines are usually good for well over 100,000 miles. I have found many RVers — who otherwise could not get into RVing

— buying class B motor homes in excellent shape. The 25-year-old class B in the upper photo has an excellent body, but you'll usually find that the small V-8 engine is at the point of needing rebuilding, and the suspension is at a point where it wanders too much. On the other hand, the 1995 class B shown in the lower photo should still be quite solid all around.

A good class C is not cheap.

A good class C (mini) takes more skill to build than a good class A. Building a class A is straightforward – like building a box with four walls, a floor, and a roof. With a class C the walls must fit the existing van front. If it has an overhead bed area, it takes intricate engineering and workmanship to get it just right. Because chassis are limited for class C's, you need to be sure that each house matches the capacity of the chassis. Although the appliances and fixtures are generally the same as in a class A, the class C's floorplan has to be planned carefully for balance. Cheapo class C's are usually thrown together without the finesse of good engineering. Like a badly designed class A, they are often hard to handle when loaded and hard to keep together. For all these reasons, a good class C will cost about as much as a cheapo class A of the same length, and just a bit less than a pretty good class A. Don't get hung up on price.

Class C motor homes can have a very low cost per mile.

I think the mini is an excellent family motor home for the reasons I mentioned before, plus it can actually give you a favorable overall cost per mile. Unlike class A's, we have a few class C brands that depreciate in the 25% to 30% range during the first five years. This, of course, is where you should be. Using the numbers for mileage costs of class A's, you can actually cut those about in half for a new class C, and to under 50 cents

a mile for an almost new one. Because most class C's have a curb weight between 6,000 and 12,000 pounds, some can be powered with small engines which can give reasonable fuel consumption. Considering space and economy, the class C is undoubtedly the most efficient type of motor home.

A good used class C isn't easy to find.

However, I am constantly amazed at the good buys available for under $10,000. I must admit that to find one in this price range, though, you'll have to spend a lot of time calling, traveling, and climbing under and over. I did this quite a few years ago for someone with a budget of $5,000. I went to the Widow's Lot in Yuma, Arizona during January and bought a 1976 mini on a Dodge chassis with a 360 engine for only $2,300. It had only 30,000 miles on the odometer and was in very good overall condition. The owner said it had bad brakes, but after we adjusted them and put on a new master cylinder (total cost of about $50), it was driven back to Washington State without any problem.

There are many class C's still in good condition from as far back as the 1970's, such as the cherry shown on this page. Most of these are on Dodge chassis with 360 or 440 engines, but they are workhorses. You'll just need to watch those wheel-

bases and GVWR's, as we'll discuss in chapter 4. In the 1980's, Chevrolet took over when Dodge discontinued building RV chassis. Chevrolet set the RVing world back by providing motor home manufacturers with truck chassis that were not adequate for motor homes. Until Ford became determined to try this volatile market in the late 1980's, RVers had to pretty much put up with Chevrolet. In spite of all the problems with Chevrolet chassis, however, some of the shorter ones do work. If your budget is under $10,000 and you are

very lucky, you might find a
Dodge or Ford still in good condition with a reasonable wheelbase and an adequate GVWR.

Many class C's of the early
1990's had some good houses.
The problem in this era was that
RVers wanted to go big, but the
chassis were still light duty. This
means that for models built before 1997, you'll find 27- and 28-
footers on chassis that have short

wheelbases and overloaded chassis. Many of these are impossible to balance and are unsafe on fast and overcrowded highways. It wasn't until 1997, when Ford came out with their
14,050-pound GVWR heavy-duty chassis, that class C builders had the opportunity to build a decently balanced mini in
lengths from 26 to 28 feet. Of course, as is normal for the RV
industry, not all class C builders opted to build on a good foundation. You will, however, find some good choices from the
1990's for almost any budget. You just have to be smart enough
to make the *right* choice.

Good used trailer coaches and fifth wheels are generally easy to find.

I've found both trailer coaches and fifth
wheels that were tremendous bargains. Complete rigs like the one shown on this page can
often be bought in the $20,000 to $30,000 range
— and that includes truck and boat. Bargains
in trailer coaches are a bit harder to find because it seems that half the families in America
are looking for a good trailer coach at the right
price. But they're available almost everywhere
in like-new condition for about 50% of the

original (new) FMV (fair market value). Because so many SUV's are being used for trailering, good trailer coaches under 25 feet long are harder to find. It's still harder to find those short trailer coaches that sleep six to eight without the need to spread air mattresses on the floor.

Small fifth wheels are common under $10,000, but the real bargains are in the larger sizes.

Because many families are looking for fifth wheels for vacation and weekend use, real bargains in used fifth wheels below 30 feet are often difficult to find. However, fifth wheels longer than 30 feet are practically everywhere at great prices. The reason is obvious: Fulltimers and snowbirds are constantly changing their minds. Quality fifth wheels from 30 to 33 feet are harder to find because they can be pulled with 3/4-ton pickups. From 33 through 36 feet you might need, at the very least, a one-ton pickup, so the demand for these long and heavy fifth wheels decreases. Generally, any fifth wheel over 36 feet will require a midsize truck — which is not as comfortable or practical for utility purposes. Because these big fifth wheels are pushed heavily by salespeople (who want "big" commissions), many buyers get carried away with the prospect of taking everything they own with them. Because the average fulltimer is active as such for less than five years, you can see why big fifth wheels around five years old can easily depreciate to 50% of the original fair-market value. Keep in mind, however, that RVs used for over 3 years of fulltiming can be quite worn out.

Worn out fold-downs are everywhere.

The problem with fold-downs is that many of them are built to self-destruct. There are only a few fold-down manufacturers who take enough pride in building these tents-on-wheels to make them last longer than it takes the kids to grow out of childhood. If you are looking for a fold-down in the Southwest — where it's dry — you

will find one more easily than those who are looking in country where it's wet most of the time. (In wet climates, all fold-downs over 5 years old are mildew-suspect.) As I mentioned in chapter 1, fold-downs take a lot of care. However, because many families change their minds about owning a fold-down almost as soon as they use it a few times, they are available almost everywhere in like-new condition. The problem is getting a good price. Most people finance their RVs for 5 to 10 years, which makes it difficult to sell within a year or two when they owe more than what it's worth on the market. Thus, the almost-new fold-downs end up on a dealer's lot because dealers know how to deal. So, if you want an almost-new fold-down for a well-used fold-down price, you'll need to be right on the ball in searching and dealing.

The photo to the right shows a trailer that isn't quite a fold-down, but for a few thousand dollars it will work for a small family, or for a couple, with a small tow vehicle. At about 1,500 pounds, it's easy on modern short-wheelbase SUV's. It's mostly a sleeper, but it's much better than a tent. I used one almost like this to make a 3-month cross-country trip in the early sixties with two youngsters. We pulled it behind a Peugeot. It's a great way to go "camping."

Telescoping trailers are scarce but available.

Because there are only a few telescoping trailer manufacturers, there are fewer of these RVs being built. With prices approximately 30% higher than for trailer coaches of comparable size, telescoping trailers are being bypassed by new buyers. I am totally amazed at how few people can see the safety in the lower profiles. Because a preconceived notion gives them the wrong message, every day people risk their lives pulling larger trailers than their tow vehicle can handle. I believe, however, that the telescoping trailer is the trailer of the future.

Properly hitched, a well-designed telescoping trailer can safely be towed with almost any vehicle. With the strong and lightweight construction techniques already available, telescoping trailers should be as durable and trouble free as good trailer coaches and fifth wheels.

The moving parts of a telescoping trailer will, of course, mean that it could have some problems down the road. Although the lift mechanism can wear, in most cases a simple adjustment should take care of any problem unless there has been extensive abuse. Keeping it simple is good, but as I will point out in chapter 4, safety is paramount.

Because many telescoping trailer owners have enjoyed the RVing experience, they move up to larger fifth wheels or motor homes. This leaves many used telescoping trailers available if you are willing to search them out. When you are considering a telescoping trailer, never expect the price to be equal to a trailer coach. They will be higher in price used, just as they are when new. An RVCG member found an almost new, top-notch 26-foot long telescoping trailer near his home. Although he needed a low profile because he was towing with an

SUV, he was tempted to pass it up because he could have bought a new trailer coach, albeit of much lower quality, for the same price. As he told me, he simply forgot about safety when he thought about price. He almost passed up a good deal because his comparisons weren't complete. Don't let this happen to you. I found the superb-looking 1983 telescoping trailer shown on this page listed on the Internet for $4,700 or best offer — much less than a cheapo new trailer would cost. When buying new or used, the price becomes important only when everything else is considered.

Chapter 3

Going to Shows
and Factories

Going to Shows and Factories

RV shows are designed to sell RVs — not promote RVs.

Many product shows are held primarily to introduce and promote various products, but not RV shows. The primary motivation for a dealer or manufacturer to be a vendor at an RV show is to sell products. Buyers need to keep this fact firmly in mind when they enter the gate. The vendors are out in force to catch you "today." They are hyped to close on every interested attendee. They are aggressively seeking buying signs. Every salesperson is on commission with little interest in "promoting" the product. The salesperson's only interest is to catch a buyer — today!

An RV show is a buyer-beware game.

Every brand and model promoted at an RV show will be touted as the best in quality and price. It will be claimed that whatever you're interested in can be driven, pulled, or carried by whatever means you have available. One way or another, every item will fit into your budget. If you just make a reasonable offer, the seller will go overboard to make you happy. If what you see isn't exactly what you want, somehow they'll make it into what you want. Just give them a deposit and the deal will be locked solid.

It's a game as old as civilization — the seller shows the wares and the buyer "bewares."

There has never been any question that the experts are the vendors and the neophytes are the buyers. This is not a game of professional against professional as in commercial shows. If you enter an RV show with the attitude that you are smarter than they are, you will be defeated. You may know more about RVs and RVing (RV salespeople in general know little about these subjects), but they know about showing and dealing. Never doubt that every dealer at an RV show will go all out to display every motor home, trailer, and camper as a precious jewel. Every model will be so dressed that it will be virtually impossible for the uninformed to distinguish the jewels from the cracker boxes.

It's rarely advantageous to buy at an RV show.

If you accept an RV show as a showplace of products, then you should be able to psych yourself into going just to look. Never go just to look and then end up buying. When lookers buy, only one deal out of ten is a good deal. It can't be good, because the buyer stops looking when the search isn't complete. The search becomes complete only when you have fully determined, on your own, which brand and model you want to buy. You must do your calculations of base price and option prices at home. Only if you know the brand and model you want, and the MSRP of that brand and model, should you entertain the idea of buying at a show. Now hear this: The dealer will have incentives for you to buy at a show (such as low financing rates), but this is rarely enough to make up for the losses you will suffer when buying unprepared. Rule: Go to the show only to look unless you are totally prepared to buy.

With these thoughts in mind, let's go on to the next page and take a walk through an RV show.

An RV show is designed to excite you and impress you. It may not be as sophisticated as Macy's front windows, but the intent is the same. After all, few people go to an RV show unless they are considering a purchase today, tomorrow, or at some time in the future.

The vendors at the show are betting that a fair number of attendees will be looking for something to buy today or tomorrow. The salespeople know that those who are very close to buying will probably buy "today" if the product is pitched right. The ones who plan on buying tomorrow or in the near future will take more skill to sell, but the show people know that a good percentage of them will also buy "today." And, don't kid yourself; at least one-third of all salespeople at RV shows are professionals at pitching the product.

Not all salespeople are bad guys. Most salespeople work hard at coming off as the common Jane or Joe. They'll give you a tidbit of information and wait for your response. There's absolutely nothing wrong with asking questions and listening to what they have to say. You simply need to remember why you're at the show.

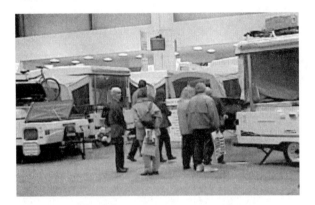

"Just walk," I tell my students when asked about avoiding contact when they don't want contact. "Load up with brochures and then look completely indifferent."

It's actually easy to do because salespeople don't want to waste time on attendees who have no interest in buying today. They want buyers, so they're looking for buying signs. If you go inside an RV, then come back out and look at an outside feature, then go back in again, the salesperson begins to pay attention. If you sit down inside as if you're testing out the furniture, the salesperson gets excited. If you open the cabinets below the sink as if to check out the storage for pots and pans, the salesperson knows that you're a potential buyer. If you start looking like you have a few questions to ask, the salesperson is right there. If you don't want the salesperson to corner you, look casual and keep walking.

If you are genuinely shopping for ideas with no intent to purchase, tell the salesperson that you're considering buying in the future, but right now you're getting ideas. Be fair. If the salesperson has the time, you'll usually get some of your questions answered anyway. Keep in mind that I said only one-third of the salespeople at RV shows are professionals. The rest are amateurs with little to offer the buyer.

If you know you are buying a specific type of RV, try to look only at that type. It's easy to get distracted from your main purpose, and then you will get tired and begin to rush. Plan the day. If there's a map of the show layout with vendors listed, use it as a check list. At the very least, go first for the type and brands you have an interest in. As you wander about the show looking for specific brands, you're bound to find some things that'll draw your attention. That's good. Stop and look a bit. There's absolutely no harm in looking and thinking — when it involves RVs, that is. The big thing to remember is that most of us start to get tired at RV shows after about six hours of wandering. I do, and I've taken enough students with me to know that six hours is about the limit. Plan at least three hours for specifics and the rest of the time for general looking. Believe me, it works better that way.

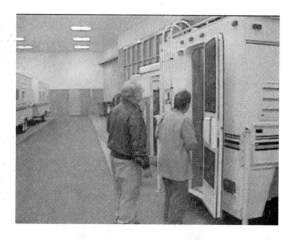

If you have a specific question for a salesperson, ask it directly. When the question is answered to your satisfaction, say, "Thank you," and walk away. Asking one question is normal, asking more than one is a buying sign. If you have more than one question, I repeat, let the salesperson know that you are just looking. If you need to, say, "I'm thinking of buying one next year." Your words and your feet need to be in sync.

Sometimes you go to a show because there are no dealers near your home who stock the brands you're considering. In this case, treat your show visitation differently. Begin with these brands while your mind and feet are fresh. Walk around the outside of the RV while looking at the profile and features. You'll probably begin to compare with those brands that you've been seeing at the dealerships. Of course, you'll want a brochure in hand so that you can make comments in it. This is the best way to keep records without spending lots of time building a system of notes.

As you walk around the RV, ask yourself whether the general appearance pleases you. It is important that the outside profile and appearance satisfy your particular tastes. You'll probably already know the rating because you've done your homework. You should find out, if you don't know, whether it's in your budget. If the ratings are good and it's in your budget, you'll want to be more attentive to details.

You might have to live with this RV for 10 years, so ask yourself a few pertinent questions about use, parking, and destinations. Avoid buying because the price is right "today."

It's often difficult to check out the exterior of a specific brand or model at a show. The way they are crammed together makes it difficult to get around all sides, climb under, and get a peek at the roof. If you become interested, get a salesperson to make a presentation. Whether you do a complete exterior check or not, it's important to check the interior. Spend some time with models and floor plans that will work for you.

You have to live with the interior once you buy it. The interior of an RV is not like the interior of a house. It's almost impossible to change once you get it home. You don't paint or paper the walls. It's difficult to change the floor covering and appliances. Because the furniture is usually built around other features, to change it means it'll never look right. If, for some reason, you need to change things, you'll have to get an idea right up front what it will entail.

You must think about your use of the RV. Will the cabinets hold the types of items you need to take with you? Will everybody using the bath be happy with the layout? There will be some compromises, but be careful about making ones you can't live with.

Rule: Never compromise at an RV show. If the interior doesn't work for you, you'll be an unhappy camper.

Never underestimate the power of a professional salesperson. As you get tired you will be more tempted to stop and listen. They'll hit you with all the wonderful things you want to hear. Remember: that's their job. They are at the show to get you into an RV. It is only through sales that they can get commissions and the dealership can pay for costs of displaying their RVs. For RV dealers to be at larger RV shows often costs between $10,000 and $25,000. They only get it back through sales. Someone has to buy sooner or later or they'll be out of business.

You are not at the RV show to keep an RV dealer in business. You're there to collect information about a potential purchase. If you need a break, start looking at incidental things like bulletin boards of used RVs. Or better still, stop for a long breather and remember why you came to the show. Reflect deep on these words: An RV show is a great place to *look*.

Next:
Visiting RV Factories

Visiting the factory can be helpful, but RV factories have their peculiarities.

In a world where so much is homogenized, it's often difficult for us to compare characteristics that appear to be greatly different. As I listen to people talk about RV tours, I begin to realize that most are influenced more by the skin than what's underneath. This is natural. We are all familiar with the skin of things, but most of us can't even conceive of the gut of things. There is much danger in judging by the skin — whether of people or things.

RV factories are designed to produce a product. Unlike an RV show, RV factories normally are not designed to sell a product. However, because so many prospective RV buyers want to see the place where their dream RV is being born, some manufacturers encourage, and even promote, factory tours. Like a watching a baby being born, watching an RV being built can have its dangers if one is not properly prepared. In a real delivery room, you must be prepared for blood, pain, and what is seemingly contradictory — ecstasy. In an RV factory you must be prepared for high activity, a sense of chaos, and your desire to believe that what you're seeing is good. You must also understand that the tourmaster's pitch — whether given by a volunteer, engineer, or super salesperson — does not necessarily reflect the finished product.

The purpose of a factory tour is to lead you down the path where all you think is — "Wonderful." Of course, it won't all be wonderful, but because you already have positive feelings about the brand, the tour need only confirm your convictions. If they put on a good show, there's a good chance you will buy the product. Most manufacturers do not rely on factory tours to keep them in business — it is another part of the promotions game.

The essence of a finished product is its long-term durability.

Regardless of your impressions of a building facility, it is the end product that will tell all. Judging solely on building techniques is never enough. I have never been able to base reliability or durability solely on watching a product being built. I have always had to rely on researching the finished product — which must include user satisfaction. You will be impressed to a degree based solely on the manufacturer's ability and desire to put on a show. This is not to say that factory tours are not important and telling, but they are far from the full story.

A factory visitation tells me what's under the skin.

There are three ways of finding out how an RV is put together: 1) study the results of accidents and complaints, 2) analyze major repairs being done on the structure, and 3) see how it's all put together during a factory tour. I do all three. However, it isn't practical for every buyer to do all or any of these. If you can do one or two with reasonable objectivity, it may help you to get some idea of the building techniques and potential deficiencies of the brand you are interested in. Of course, when I go to an RV factory I do not normally take the standard factory tour. I am usually allowed to wander freely and take pictures. It's understandable that the builder can't let just anyone wander about without some supervision, so don't expect too much freedom. But you will be allowed to ask questions and, I hope, you will get some good answers. However, you will probably not be allowed to take pictures. Whether you take the official factory tour or make it a special visitation, don't expect too much. This type of activity is time consuming for factory personnel and can detract from the regular business of building RVs.

Now, let's take a look at what I have seen during a variety of factory visitations.

Taking a factory tour, like going to an RV show, can be fraught with danger for the unwary. If you have no idea what you are in for, and if you have not done your initial research on the quality of the manufacturer, you could be wasting time. Because most people are easily influenced by what they see and hear, I usually recommend taking factory tours of only those brands that you have previously considered acceptable. However, if you are the type of person who needs broad education, with all the risks that go with it, then jump in and take whatever comes.

Some factories are large, some are small. In RV factories you'll probably find a small business office removed from the main facility. This is where you'll meet the tourmaster. The size or the outside appearance of the factory, or complex of factories, rarely tells you anything about the quality of the RVs being built under the roof — whether it is the worst or the best. I learned the hard way that, like the RV itself, quality is deep under the skin. If you have your heart set on a specific brand or manufacturer, try not to make judgements up front. Don't go with the idea that you're going to learn everything about the manufacturing process. Simply

resolve to watch for the overall attitudes and the attention-to-detail of management and workers, and learn what you can about building techniques. Before you enter the door to begin your tour, remember to take a deep breath and open your mind. Be ready for some surprises.

Once I'm inside, I quickly scan the complete facility with no special purpose except to get an initial impression. However, I don't have to get in very far before I begin to enjoy the activity of the assembly process. As I'm half listening to what the tourmaster is saying, I allow my eyes to take in more than my ears. This is the time to let any biases or expectations take the back seat. This is a time to get first impressions — to observe and enjoy.

I always try to look at the chassis first. After all, the chassis is the foundation of the RV. If the chassis isn't done right, the RV won't be right. If the manufacturer has its own chassis department, I like to see it being put together. If the chassis is not built in-shop, if it's subletted, I want to study the finished product in detail.

I always study trailer chassis very closely. Unlike motor home chassis, trailer chassis are often put together with little engineering and a lot of welding. In the factories where the chassis shown on this page were built, the welding was excellent and they even used good engineering techniques. I watch closely to see how accessories, like the slideout room motors, are installed. The attention-to-detail here is extremely important.

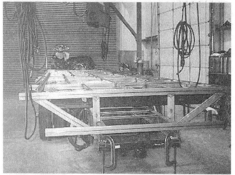

I treat motor home chassis a bit differently than trailer chassis. If the chassis is purchased from a chassis manufacturer, I already know much about it. I have studied up on the manufacturer before coming to the factory. I think I know what to expect, but I want to see how the house is applied to the chassis.

If the motor home manufacturer builds its own chassis, I will treat it much like a trailer chassis. I like to see it all come together. I want to see the raw material and the welding. It's usually fascinating.

Because I'm a curious person, I study every detail. I crawl under and over until the tourmaster begins to get nervous.

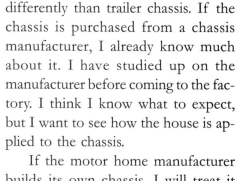

When you've laid the foundation you'd better start thinking about the floor — just as you would with a house. I've seen so many different ways that floors are put onto trailer and motor home chassis that sometimes I wonder if there are any standard techniques. Some flooring supports are built from steel, some from aluminum, and others from wood. Some manufacturers use fewer but heavier pieces; some use straightforward techniques while focusing on attention-to-detail; and some get downright fancy and sell heavily on their "engineered" features.

I like to watch how they structure the floor for durability — for at least 20 years of hard use. I focus on materials like the flooring — plywood or oriented strand board (OSB)? Tongue and groove or straight edge? Screwed and glued or nailed? Protected against plumbing and roof leaks? Structured for the average floor load, or good enough for those well over 200 pounds? All these questions are relevant when watching floors being assembled.

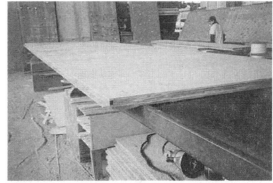

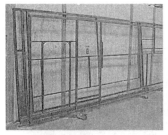

Whether the framing is made of wood or metal, the wall structure is extremely important. Although most motor homes are built with steel or aluminum today, there are some who still use wood. The same goes for trailers — whether fifth wheels or trailer coaches. I have found that if the wall is built with good engineering techniques, good material, and good workmanship, it makes little difference in reliability or durability whether the framing is wood or metal.

When I visit an RV factory, I know in advance the brand's strengths and weaknesses. This helps me look deeper and with eyes wide open. Like I've said before, though, it's important to keep an open mind.

Insulation is especially important to trailer buyers. Well, it may also be important to motor home buyers, but it shouldn't be as important because motor homes are generally not designed for subfreezing weather and, in spite of insulation, they are difficult to heat and cool in hot or cold climates. Anyway, it is interesting to watch the different techniques of applying insulation.

Some insulation is foam, laminated into the structure. Some is fiberglass mat held in place with a bit of glue. And, in some RVs the treated insulation sheets are hand-laid under the skin. Even though most techniques work well if the workmanship is sound, they are not equal. It is absolutely clear that some applications work better for certain use classifications. I am especially conscious of techniques that improve the structural integrity, like foam board, while improving the RV's ability to stay warm or cool —as required by the climate.

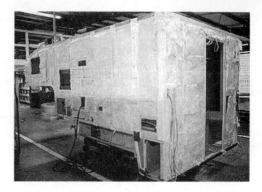

Pressure- and vacuum-bonding are processes that make for strong wall, floor, and roof structures. Pressure-bonding has been around for over 20 years, and vacuum-bonding has been used in some RVs for about 15 years. Pressure-bonding has been pretty much trouble free, but air-quality controls have made it difficult to continue in some states. Vacuum-bonding is a laminating process that has worked well with some manufacturers and has been disastrous with others. It all comes down to good quality control.

When I first started visiting motor home factories, the vacuum-bonding process consisted of putting the assembly in one vacuum table. Now they're often stacked four high. If you get a chance to watch the vacuum-bonding process while at a factory, do so. It's very interesting.

Cages are very important to motor home safety. The cage is the metal structure that surrounds the motor home. A pure cage is built first and then the interior wall is structured onto it. A modern-day process is vacuum-bonding the steel structure into the wall structure. Although this is not a pure cage, I believe it can be as effective as a cage if the structure and the bonding process are adequate to keep the vehicle from disintegrating if involved in a rollover accident.

When I go to a factory, checking out the cage or wall structure in detail is a priority whether it's a motor home or a trailer. I have seen too many deficiencies in this area to treat it with a ho-hum attitude. If it's metal, I want to see the strength of the tubing and the quality of the fastening — whether welded, screwed, or bolted. Even if made of wood, I want to know the weaknesses. There is much riding on the strength of the house structure — especially surrounding the cockpit in class A motor homes.

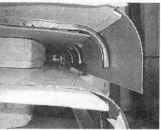

Of course, once the floor and walls are in place with the house structure pretty much complete, it's about time to install some sort of roof. Oh my, how I like to see the roof being assembled, raised into the air, lightly dropped onto the existing structure, fastened into place, and covered — with whatever. The roof is very important — if it leaks everything seems to fall apart. Good manufacturers treat the roof as if it's the heart of the RV.

I want to know everything I can about the roof covering. Whether it's fiberglass, rubber, or metal, the quality of materials and workmanship is paramount to a good RV. If there's a weakness in the roof, I need to find it. To do that, I need to carefully study the entire assembly process.

There are two ways of structuring the interior: You can build the interior onto the floor and then put on the walls; or you can build the structure, then install the interior.

Regardless of the sequence, one thing we have learned is very important: The interior cabinets and partitions must be securely fastened to the wall, floor, *and* roof. We are finding out from the results of accidents that the interior of the RV is most important because it supports the walls in case of a rollover. As you study the process at the factory, don't just look at the woodworking — look at how it's all tied through the main structure. Walking around the unfinished structure will give you a good chance to see how the cabinets are fastened into the wall and what they are fastened to. If cabinets are simply fastened to paneling, don't expect the structure to be solid.

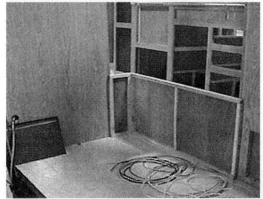

After the floor, walls, and roof, are attached, slideout rooms are added. They are an adjunct to the RV in that they are not essential. Because they are added rooms, you must look at them for what they may do to the durability, reliability, and longevity of the RV.

The impact of slideout rooms on the structural integrity of the house is extremely important. It is important to examine the support material for the large cutout. The type of mechanism used to operate the slideout is also something to study. How the slideout and the mechanism work together (being that they are integral to the house) cannot be ignored. If you are planning on an RV with a slideout room, you should be very interested in looking at all the components that make up this feature.

Never miss the installation of utilities. Good electrical, plumbing, and ducting engineering and installation are extremely important to the overall reliability of the RV. Utility problems are the number one cause of frustrations. And the RV lifestyle does not need frustrations.

Because there are few standards in the RV industry, there are many different techniques used for installing the many components needed for proper plumbing, wiring, ducting, and liquid storage. With every factory tour, I see something different. Sometimes it's the material. Sometimes it's the way it's put together. The tourmaster will invariably talk about the advantages of their current techniques and why their methods are better than those used by their competitors. The tourmaster may concede that they have had problems in the past, but those problems have now been eliminated with these new techniques. This is as good a time as any to nod and take it with a grain of salt. It is simply one part of a whole.

Once the walls are on and the interior is installed, the work still isn't done. There is a lot of finishing and checking to be performed. Finishing touches include finding things that were not done correctly. They must not include covering up mistakes. As those who have long lists of defects after the purchase have told me, "Mistakes should have been caught and corrected at the factory."

Because an RV is a complicated structure, it's important that there be a good quality-control person at the end of the line. As you take in this part of the process, look for the little things that you think should have been caught. See how many you can find in just a few minutes.

As you take the last steps in your factory tour, check out the finished product that will be delivered to the dealer. With the assembly process fresh in your mind, you will probably see things in a different light.

To reiterate what I said at the beginning of the tour, you must always keep in mind that the way it looks at the factory and on the sales lot is not the final word. The real judgement must be based on performance.

Conclusion: RV shows and factory tours can be helpful.

The RV show can be useful in "kicking off" the research, and the factory tour can help you make a final decision. It won't work for you to use a factory tour for basic research or a show for making your choice. You need to know the manufacturer's reputation for handling complaints and the brand's record for reliability. You need to know if the model under consideration will satisfy your needs. In essence, it takes good analysis combined with astute observation to reduce the risk of buying a bad RV.

I'd like to leave you with an important message about manufacturers and dealers in general. They are, above all, people like you and me. They are, much like you and me, caught up in some sort of machine that tells them what to do and how to do it. Even though the machine itself may not be to our liking, the individuals — who are, in essence, the gears of this machine — are just performing their jobs. They turn as they are told to turn. It is the controlling gears that often need to be replaced. If a machine is putting out a bad product, the controlling gears can be blamed. For that reason, be understanding of those who are simply doing their jobs.

This is not to excuse the few people in many organizations or companies who are downright unfair, corrupt, ruthless, rude, greedy, indifferent, and ignorant. I have seen it all in my long life, and I can assure you that the RV industry has its share of such people. Because of a few, however, we can never justify treating the other 95% like they are one of *those*. Until you are absolutely sure, I urge you to give everyone you meet who is filling the role of an RV professional the benefit of the doubt.

Chapter 4

Being Safe
and Legal

Being Safe and Legal

"Safety is relative to personal philosophy," I was told by one who scoffed at my advocacy for safer RVs.

"Some of us don't need it," he continued.

"You are right, safety is relative. It's relative to life and death," I replied. "But because RV safety involves everyone on the highway, it goes beyond personal philosophy."

I fight the battle every day. Manufacturers are especially defensive, but we also have many RVers who think that civil liberties involve the right to drive an unsafe RV. Of course there are the silent ones: RVers who bury their heads in the sand because they can't envision an accident happening to them. Then there are those wonderful few who believe they can change the world and are willing to try. They keep us going, and sometimes they fight with us. Being on the front lines is never for the weak.

I am concerned about the RV safety issue because I am part of it.

I am also concerned because I have been shocked by the results of accidents. Because I believe there are 100 similar accidents for every one I see, I simply multiply the result by 100. When a family was wiped out by losing the brakes of a new motor home on a Montana mountain, I had a dream in which I saw hundreds of bodies scattered across the terrain with piles of debris from broken class A's scattered in a ravine. The terrible cries of pain from the dying were worse than the worst scene from a modern-day violent movie. The terrible sadness and agony of those who loved the victims were part of my own agony. It was too much. Although I know such accidents still happen, I can say with confidence that much of the blame for these disasters lies in the indifference of our government agencies and the general public.

I think what upset me most was that the vehicle involved in the aforementioned accident was deemed unsafe in *The RV Ratings Guide CD* at least one year prior to the accident. It was deemed unsafe because the manufacturer of that motor home is a sloppy RV builder and should be put out of business. This manufacturer cheats on chassis capacity, cheats on workmanship, and cheats on giving out solid information. This manufacturer knows what it is doing: That grandparents are trusting enough to take their grandchildren with them in their big class A motor homes. If the tobacco industry can be judged liable for killing thousands of people because of its indifference, then surely RV manufacturers should be held to a code of ethics in their manufacturing and promotions activities.

> *RV manufacturers should be held to a code of ethics in their manufacturing and promotions activities.*

What I have just told you is a small part of the reason why I do what I do. You may not like my hard-hitting approach, but it is the only way I know to get the job done. I have tried the soft approach. I spent years talking to manufacturers. I have talked to the various state and federal agencies. It has all been to no avail. In my last years I can do no more than take my message to the people. However, if you are squeamish about knowing the facts of the safety and legal aspects of RVs, or if you think that I've been negative in the previous three chapters, I urge you to skip this chapter and go directly to The Walkabout.

The biggest danger is buying big.

"What?" you say, "how can bigger be less safe?" The answer is simple: The bigger the heavier. Big motor homes are generally structurally the same as small motor homes. They contain more mass and more weight. Therefore, if you run into a moose on a Maine road with a big class A motor home, you'll find a moose in your lap as quickly as you will in a smaller one. However, if you hit a big object with a big RV — whether motor home or vehicle with trailer— it won't stop as fast as a smaller one. In a rollover situation, the weight of the chassis on most big class A's — such as the one shown on this page — will crumble the walls and roof. Not a pretty picture, but if you are safety conscious, this is something you must consider.

Size can open up a "legal" can of worms.

Length is generally not a problem unless you plan on exceeding 40 feet. Some states are moving toward limiting motor home size on their highways to 40 feet in length — which makes RVers driving 40- to 45-footers very unhappy. In California, you need a class B license to drive a motor home over 40 feet — and motor homes over 45 feet are not allowed. Whether enactment and enforcement holds up in the near future, I believe that we'll see some major modifications made to existing length limitations for federal and state highways very early in the twenty-first century. If you exceed existing limitations, you will be subject to citations that will bring penalties. If you are involved in an accident when your RV is oversize, regardless of fault, you may also find yourself facing a serious lawsuit. If your RV is close to any highway size limitations, be sure you understand the legal restrictions imposed on traffic for the highways that you will be traveling.

A widebody often plays with the law.

Although it is a wonderful feature for fulltiming and snowbirding, there is ongoing controversy over 102-inch-wide RVs. The RV industry implies that these widebodies are okay to take just about anywhere you want. The words we need to look at here are "okay," and "just about." This is all salesperson talk to make it sound safe and legal. I'm sure you won't find a written statement saying that it's completely legal to drive anywhere in North America with a widebody RV — because it isn't. It is clearly written in federal statutes that no vehicle driving on federal roads can exceed the 102-inch width — except for safety devices, such as rear-view mirrors. There has been no exclusion for protrusions such as awnings. Therefore, awnings that extend the width of the vehicle to more than 102 inches are illegal in most states.

It is also clear that many states prohibit wide vehicles on some roads. And in case you're not afraid to take a chance on getting a fine, there's always the question of liability if the vehicle is involved in an accident. Although this legal issue has not been openly discussed or enforced by various government agencies, you need to be aware that it does exist and that things can change at any time.

Stability is a big motor home problem.

Stability in motor homes has to do with wheelbase, weight, and balance. You will want to study all three if you have any concern for control of your RV at highway speeds. If you want your RV to forgive your mistakes, it has to rate high in these three characteristics. Wheelbase will keep you on a straight path. Weight will determine how well you stop. Balance at the four corners will determine how well the RV will respond to adverse road conditions. This may be oversimplified, but if you remember it this way, it will be a good beginning.

And I'm not leaving big trailers off the hook either.

Too-big trailers being towed by too-small SUV's or trucks are a menace to everyone on the highway — including themselves. Towing a 38- to 40-foot fifth wheel with a one-ton pickup is tantamount to playing Russian roulette because there's no reserve for stopping or control. The story is even worse for those SUV's towing 28-foot trailer coaches. Even though the chance of survival is better for the occupants of towing vehicles, the accident rate is too high. We need to do a better job at matching house to chassis and towing vehicle to trailer.

Design deficiencies are to blame for most of the problems that surface with trailer coaches and fifth wheels.

The biggest problem with travel trailers in general, and trailer coaches in particular, is that anyone can build them. If you have a barn or big shed, you can buy all the components and put them together like the erector toys we used to play with as kids. If you can build enough of them, you can set yourself up with a dealer network to push them on the market. If you do a pretty good job, and especially if they look good, you will probably sell every one. You can't bake and sell cookies without mucho permits, but in many states building and selling RVs is like taking candy from a baby.

Towing a 38- to 40-foot fifth wheel with a one-ton pickup is tantamount to playing Russian roulette . . . there's no reserve for stopping or control.

Protection in case of an accident should always be a concern.

As an advocate of the RVing lifestyle, I must even question myself as to what is happening in accident avoidance and occupant protection. To stay objective I am forced to look back in my history and into the history of the class A to see if the problems with this type of RV have always existed, or if something has happened to change the dynamics of the whole picture from 1970 to date. Because no government agency cares about the RV industry as we know it, data relating to numbers, causes, and results of RV accidents is skimpy at best. One reason for this is that highway police know very little about RVs. When I studied accident report forms, I was shocked to find that there was, and still is, almost nothing to help establish RV accident statistics. An accident report might mention that it's a motor home or trailer, but it rarely differentiates between types. Sometimes there will be a mention of brand or manufacturer, but rarely both. I've never seen "model" mentioned, even though it is the most telling bit of information needed for research. Because of this lack of basic information, the facts concerning deficiencies in the manufacturing of RVs can never be extracted from existing government databases. Maybe the indifference of the general public stems from a sense of hopelessness in that "we can't fight city hall." I think the situation is far from hopeless — if consumers aggressively demand that manufacturers build RVs with safety in mind, and that all new RVs be tested for crashworthiness.

There are indicators that bring questions of accident survivability into focus.

For example, in an analysis of Washington State's records on motor home accidents, there appears to be three deaths for every 100 people involved. This data considers every accident — even fender benders. Because the data reflects only a few years, a few hundred accidents, and is from only one source, I cannot consider it as solid. But the information is solid enough to get me thinking about the subject of survivability. Are you willing to take a 3% risk of dying if you are involved in an accident? I don't think you would be if this number were absolutely solid. But what if the risk were even higher? What if the overall risk of a particular type were 5%? What if your age made the risk closer to 10%? If you feel that these numbers are relevant when you are choosing the type of RV for your great travel adventures, you must consider the ramifications of the wrong choice. You must ask yourself questions like the one posed by the photo: Will the driver be safe with that large TV over his/her head? Although it is proven unsafe to my satisfaction, how do you feel about it?

You won't find accident victims on the trail.

There are few RVers congregating in campgrounds or attending seminars who have been involved in serious RV accidents. Those few are usually quiet and subdued about the details because they know others don't want to hear about them. They are now resigned to the fact that RVing, like climbing Mount Everest, has some serious risks. They were the unlucky ones. A few accident victims may continue in the lifestyle — but will surely be more careful.

We need to take the initiative.

RVing is too important to those of us involved in it not to have a continuing advocacy for safety. But it is a lot of work. A good advocacy program must clearly identify the problems and focus on possible solutions. This is why good information needs to be collected and published. It is always the hope of any advocacy program that the collection of seeds will eventually result in an abundant harvest. Because of RV Consumer Group, a harvest has been realized.

Class A's dominated my learning years.

Although I began trailering in 1957, I got into my first motor home in 1963. I built it from an Air Force bus. It was only 28 feet long but it served us well for 15 years. My first

family traveled the country twice in this motor home and lived in it about 30% of the time. Later, Connie and I added the trailer, which became a photo lab and writing studio (upper photo). In the late 1970's, we built another custom motor home from a Crown school bus, with which we pulled our heavy-weather sailboat. This is a very safe class A with a long wheelbase. It is structured like a tank. (Lower photo shows my beautiful mother-in-law Maria, our sailboat *Periwinkle*, and our converted motor home in the background. We still have this motor home, although it is retired and serves mostly as a storage facility.) We later bought a 25-foot trailer as an auxiliary unit, and in the early 1980's we bought a 31-foot factory-built class A so shoddy in workmanship and structural integrity that it set the course for establishing RV Consumer Group.

I learned a lot about RVs with my first and only factory-built class A. I kept it for three years and sold it for pretty much what I paid for it. I then entered the RV arena professionally and really started learning. In 1988, when I started teaching and writing about RVing, I quickly learned about the differences in RV types, brands, and models. I soon saw the importance of making the right choice — beginning with type. Early in the 1990's I began to look critically at the class A — which eventually led me into a complete study of RV safety.

We must face the fact that most class A's are judged unsafe by automobile standards.

We know that many class A's are involved in collisions, rollovers, and fires — and that in no way can you be exempted as a potential victim. Any or all of the three may be waiting for you around the next corner or over the next hill. Although you need to be prepared for accidents at any time in any type of vehicle, with a motor home you need to know that there are few regulations — in fact almost none — in the building of an RV. This means that airplanes, autos, and commercial buses may be scrutinized by various agencies for safety aspects, but RVs are not. Even the few controls that are in force — like those concerning electric and fire safety — are barely regulated and enforced. The RV industry is almost totally unregulated.

A simple question you must ask is, "If I am driving my class A and I am forced off the road into a utility pole or tree, how am I and my passengers protected if I hit the obstacle at 30 miles per hour?" The answers are also simple: Most class A's have no low-speed bumpers, no reasonable frontal crush area, little impact absorption, and no external fire-spread controls. They have no mandatory controls for passenger protection behind the cockpit. There are no recommendations, guidelines, or mandated building techniques for rollover integrity. It's all left up to the manufacturers. If an RV comes completely apart during a rollover, the manufacturer cannot be cited in any way. There are no stipulations anywhere that motor homes must be built to survive a rollover, to protect the occupants in a collision at 30 miles-per-hour, or to keep fires from spreading so fast that

occupants have no time to escape. The upper photo shows the lack of a low-speed collision bar in a $150,000 motor home. The lower photo shows what can happen in a class A rollover accident. Because there are no mandatory controls for collision or rollover protection, the various agencies tell us that it's up to consumers to control the industry through purchasing power and the courts. As in the days of the Wild West, we must rely on the RV community to protect itself. Very simply: Your level of protection is in your choice of RV.

We know beyond question that some class A motor home brands disintegrate during a rollover or collision. This means they come completely apart. When the walls fall off, the occupants fly out. We know the root cause of this is design deficiency. We know that the engineers normally employed in the RV industry have little knowledge of structural integrity in accident scenarios because they are not trained to look at the negative aspects of RV building. The RV industry emphasizes only the positive side of RVing — leaving the negative aspects for the consumers to worry about.

Of course, not all class A's come completely apart during a rollover. Right now, though, it looks like about 50% of them do. We even know some of the reasons why. Although this research is in its infancy, the evidence points strongly toward specific deficiencies in building and design techniques. As the evidence mounts in the 21st century, I hope there will be some changes made to improve the situation.

Another danger with big class A's has to do with highway control.

According to *The RV Ratings Guide CD,* the bulk of class A's over 35 feet long have short wheelbases and overloaded chassis. This is a sad situation that could be corrected by the RV industry, but it hasn't been, and it probably won't be in the near future. There's too much money to be made in selling big and cheap to change methods of building and promoting. You, as the buyer, must research thoroughly before you spend. It's the only way to get yourself into a relatively safe motor home.

Wheelbase is a major problem in motor home design.

There is no question that without a good wheelbase your RV will have a tendency to wander all over the road — even under normal conditions. Under adverse conditions, a short

There is no question that without a good wheelbase your RV will have a tendency to wander all over the road — even under normal conditions.

wheelbase motor home will have a tendency to carry you off the road. This is proven by basic laws of physics and by many testimonials of RVers who have been scared beyond belief by out-of-control motor homes. We know for a fact that any motor home with a wheelbase-to-length ratio under 54% can easily take all control out of your hands. Even with this indisputable fact, many manufacturers are still building motor homes with wheelbases below 50% wheelbase-to-length ratio. This should make you wonder whether they have any concern for your safety, or whether they know what they are doing.

Diesel pushers are long because wheelbase is the limiter.

The nature of the diesel pusher requires that the engine be behind the rear axles. To have an adequate wheelbase with such a configuration, you need at least 36 feet of overall length. Although there's a controversy over balance that relates to front and rear overhang, I stick to a 54% wheelbase-to-length ratio as a minimum for good control under adverse conditions for any motor home. Even with this minimum, balance must be at an optimum. I am not squeamish about advocating that the qualifications for any good motor home begin with a good wheelbase and good balance. Less than this increases the risk of accident. When you start thinking of class A's, whether pusher or puller, you need to think of chassis characteristics and dimensions.

I stick to a 54% wheelbase-to-length ratio as a minimum for good control under adverse conditions for any motor home.

High-end class A's may offer more safety.

High-end motor homes may be built on commercial bus chassis and shells. This means that the chassis and general structures are built like commercial buses. These are generally good in both frontal crush area and rollover strength. New ones are also extremely expensive. A used one about 15 years old usually sells for about the price you would pay for a new entry-level class A. For many, used is the way to go. If you don't mind spending a bit of time and money on upkeep, you

might want to look for a bus conversion. With the right engine and the right chassis, you can live and drive in luxury without spending a fortune.

The photo on this page shows a diesel pusher bus conversion that is about 20 years old. Notice the long wheelbase and imagine the structure of a commercial bus. If you are generally concerned with safety and you want a class A, something like this might be a logical choice. It won't be new, so it might take some maintenance; but, when considering all things, it might be a good option for those to whom safety is paramount.

Weight is a major problem.

Although RV Consumer Group explains payload on the *RV Ratings Guide CD*, I want to address it briefly here. With class A's, payload must not be a ho-hum subject. It is serious because at least 40% of all class A's are deficient in payload according to minimum standards — and many more may be deficient for snowbirding and fulltiming use.

Payload is an integral part of the chassis because it is the difference between the capacity of the chassis and the weight of the entire motor home. Because "payload" is really a commercial term, we have converted the term for RVs to "personal payload" to make it a bit easier to understand. Personal payload is the weight of persons, personal supplies, and equipment that you can load without exceeding the capacity of the chassis. Although personal items vary greatly with RVers, a good average is 1,000 pounds for vacationing, 1,500 pounds for snowbirding, and at least 2,000 pounds for fulltiming — based on two occupants. The 2,000 pounds for fulltiming is more often exceeded than the weights shown for the other uses, with some fulltimers carrying as much as 3,000 pounds of personal goods. Meeting or even exceeding these numbers, however, is not a problem if the RV has sufficient payload capacity.

How do you know if the RV has enough capacity for your personal items?

First of all, you need to know how much the motor home weighs before it's loaded with you, your passengers, and all your personal gear and supplies needed for your adventure. Then figure the maximum weight you will be loading, because you cannot exceed the capacity of the chassis. If the vehicle's capacity is not great enough, you will need to be careful not to compromise in a way that can cost you your life.

So let's get back to the formula. First, the chassis capacity (gross vehicle weight rating, or GVWR for short); second, the curb weight (the actual weight of the motor home with fuel and fresh water tanks full; third, the weight you will be loading in persons and personal supplies. Now, take the GVWR, subtract the curb weight, and subtract the weight of persons and supplies. What you have left is a weight reserve to act as a safety buffer for brakes and suspension. Now, let's take one factor at a time.

Formula	
	GVWR
minus	**Curb Weight (w/water & fuels)**
minus	**the weight of persons and personal items you load**
equals	**the weight reserve to act as a safety buffer.**

GVWR is the capacity of the chassis.

This means that the brakes and suspension are built to support the total load as designated by this number. Thus if the GVWR is 20,000 pounds, the total weight of the vehicle must never exceed this amount. This is a legal and liability issue, so keep it firmly in mind. Remember, it is the capacity of brakes and suspension — components that control the stopping and steering. If you exceed the GVWR, you will seriously increase the accident risk because you will not have control as designed into the chassis. By law, staying within the GVWR is the responsibility of the driver.

Many motor home manufacturers do not seriously consider GVWR when they decide to put a specific house on a specific chassis. Theoretically, as long as they do not exceed the GVWR of the chassis when the motor home leaves the factory, they may not be held legally responsible for violations of "highway" law. Because of this they are often lax on how close they get to the GVWR when they put a house on a chassis. Consumer law may look at this issue differently, but this is normally resolved by the courts. If, as the driver, you want to stay clear of violating "highway" law, you must be sure that you do not allow the loading of the vehicle to exceed the gross vehicle weight rating.

The more there is, the more difficult it will be to keep in balance.

Balance and axle ratings are also very important.

To understand balance, it's necessary to understand a bit more about GVWR. You see, GVWR is the total capacity of all axles. The gross axle weight rating (GAWR) is the capacity of each axle assembly. The GAWR tells you how much each axle assembly can carry and stop. So, if you add the two GAWR's together (or possibly three if there's a tag axle), you should have the GVWR. However, because the chassis components also include the chassis rails and connections between the axle assemblies, a manufacturer may reduce the GVWR from that total. That is why, sometimes, you may find the GVWR is less than the total of the GAWR's. Never, however, should the GVWR exceed the total of the GAWR's.

Balance has to do with the amount of load on each set of axles and each wheel. If a motor home is correctly balanced, it should ride and steer evenly. If you have more weight by percentage of capacity on the front axle than the rear, you will be out-of-balance. For example, if you have a 17,000- pound

GVWR, you will probably have a 6,000-pound GAWR on the front and an 11,000-pound GAWR on the rear. If you weigh the motor home and the weight at the rear axle is 10,700 pounds, that's 97% of the GAWR of 11,000 pounds. If the weight at the front axle is 5,100 pounds, that's 85% of the GAWR of 6,000 pounds. Because the difference of 12% between 97% and 85% is substantial, the load should be shifted to put another 500 pounds forward. You can do the same with each wheel.

Many times it is almost impossible for the driver to balance a motor home because the engineering was bad to begin with. If the fresh water tank is not just forward of the rear axle, the balance will be upset as the amount of water changes. If the black and gray water holding tanks are too far forward or too far to the rear, the balance can be upset as those amounts change. The same goes for side to side. You can see from this that it is critical that a motor home manufacturer be good at engineering if the vehicle is to stop and steer well under normal and adverse road conditions.

Many motor home manufacturers do not seriously consider GVWR when they decide to put a specific house on a specific chassis.

Many manufacturers show the weights on a label in the motor home.

Although the weights shown are not always clear and precise, their presence is a sign of things changing for the better. In this voluntary weight-labeling program you will usually see that the weight is given as unloaded vehicle weight (UVW). Some manufacturers subtract the UVW from the GVWR and show the difference as net carrying capacity (NCC) — a few show it as GCC for gross carrying capacity. These numbers are supposed to tell you what you need to know, but they don't. Here's why: Although the UVW does include fuel, it does not include propane, fresh water, and dealer-installed options — to get you to "curb" weight. If you want to get an estimated curb weight, you will need to add the weights of propane, fresh water and dealer-installed options to the UVW. Again, when you know the curb weight, you can subtract it from the GVWR to determine your personal payload.

You will most probably see the term CCC (Cargo Carrying Capacity) on the labels or in the brochures. This is nothing more than the personal payload as defined above less the amount of sleeping spaces multiplied by 154 (average person's weight). Don't let the CCC shock you too much, but it is a good indicator of how much personal payload you will have left if you travel with all occupants positions and tanks full.

A motor home is like a house — it needs a good foundation.

A good foundation on a motor home means having a good chassis with a house to match. Although this matching is quite a technical accomplishment, it is not difficult to find out if the job has been done properly. You simply need to weigh the entire RV, then each axle separately, and each wheel separately. When you have these numbers, simply subtract these weights from the GAWR and the GVWR numbers that must be furnished to you by the RV manufacturer. If you do this before and after you load for your first expedition, you will know whether you are headed for trouble down the road from being overloaded at any place on the foundation.

A good foundation also means that there is built-in stability. The primary factors in travel stability are balance, braking, and wheelbase. A good foundation also means a good reputation for structural integrity by the chassis manufacturer. Not all chassis have a reputation for having the strength needed to keep plugging along for a hundred-thou-

It all begins with the foundation.

sand miles and 20 years. Some chassis have been produced that have close to 25%   failure within the first
five years. You don't want this kind of foundation on
your motor home. Even if you can afford the risk in dollars, you can't afford the risk of an accident.

So, before you get excited about any motor home
brand or model, do your research on chassis. You can do
most of it yourself — try the Internet.

In summary of class A motor homes:

Class A's can be relatively safe. Some are, but sadly
many are not. This strong opinion has been formulated by experience and observation. However, there *are* good alternatives.

Class B's can provide a safe mode of RVing.

Because class B motor homes are built on standard van
chassis, they are likely to be relatively safe if they are properly
designed and modified. Class B's are designed and built by the
van manufacturer with criteria for low-speed and moderate-
speed collision. They are also designed to withstand certain
rollover stresses in the structure, which may be either weak-
ened or strengthened by the RV modifier. It is important to
realize, however, that all protection behind the cockpit is at
the discretion of the RV manufacturer. For this reason you
need to study carefully any modifications to the sidewalls and
roof, the installation of cabinets and other fixtures, and the
fastenings of passenger restraints behind the cockpit. Although
I have seen some apparent deficiencies in these areas, for the
most part, I consider class B's about as safe as a sedan.

> *Class B's are designed
> and built by the van
> manufacturer with
> criteria for low-speed
> and moderate-speed
> collision.*

A well-structured class C may be the only safe and practical motor home for most families.

I have preached this for years, and as I study the accident reports, I am constantly reinforcing the premise that a well-built class C is the ideal family motor home. A well-structured class C without a slideout room can be designed to satisfy any family's needs. For over 20 years the class C has been the motor home of the American family. Although a class B might work for the small family, most Americans eventually complain about not having enough space.

I consider the class C a generally safe bet if it is built by a quality-conscious manufacturer. You must remember that the house of a class C motor home is totally constructed by the builder. It is not like most of the class B's that leave the van walls intact. Also, it is important to realize that class C's are usually designed to carry as many as six passengers. If the house structure is not properly designed and constructed, it can literally fly apart during a rollover. There are no federal or state codes for motor home construction to protect passengers seated behind the driver. The government does not care whether a motor home comes completely apart by just falling onto its side, or if it holds together after a big tumble. It's all left up to the buyer to make a good selection and for the courts to punish, after the fact, if the manufacturer gets too sloppy. It's the way our system works. I'm telling you this because I like the class C. But if you buy a bad one — and there are some bad ones — all bets are off.

Overloaded class C's can be dangerous.

Class C's with too short wheelbases and overloaded chassis are unwieldy and difficult to handle under normal conditions, and are dangerous under adverse road conditions. Either problem by itself is bad — together they can be disastrous. The photo on this page shows a long class C with a slideout room. Many of these models are longer than 30 feet, and with the Ford 14,050-pound GVWR van cutaway chassis, they have little or no payload. This means stopping and handling will be marginal at best. Now imagine hooking a boat to the motor home. Unless the boat is perfectly braked and hitched, handling characteristics will deteriorate further. An extensive study of the subject is required by anyone who is planning on going 30 feet or longer with a van-chassis class C.

The trailer coach is the most unforgiving of RVs.
Because so many manufacturers build them, the quality of trailer coaches varies up and down the scale more than any other RV type. It seems that anyone can build a trailer coach and sell it. A barn or an old deserted cement plant can easily be used for trailer manufacturing. All one needs to do is buy the chassis and axles, install a floor, build four walls and a roof, order some appliances and fixtures from a catalogue, and — presto! — you've got a saleable product — no government approval required. Any carpenter can build a crackerbox RV. Good quality RVs, however, are as difficult to engineer and build as any good vehicle. If all RV buyers knew the difference between good quality and crackerbox RV's, there wouldn't be any crackerbox RVs.

Many RVers don't consider safety when purchasing a trailer coach because you tow it — you don't ride in it. They don't know that a poorly-designed trailer coach is uncontrollable on the highway. They don't know that when it flips, it can flip the tow vehicle as well. They don't know that at least 50% of all trailer coaches built have a tendency to wobble, sway, and flip. They don't know that most RV manufacturers don't have engineers who understand the dynamics of trailering. Buying a trailer coach without extensive research is foolhardy and dangerous.

If Charlotte can do it right, you can do it right!

You can tow a trailer coach with a sedan or an SUV. Not all trailers, however, should be towed behind any vehicle. You need the proper vehicle and the proper hitching device to tow a trailer properly and safely. One of RVCG's founders, Charlotte Landolt, travels extensively every year in her SUV while towing a 15-foot trailer coach. Even though she keeps the trailer well balanced, she is careful about hitching — as illustrated on this page.

You simply cannot afford to make a mistake when you set up to tow a trailer coach. You must search for one that perfectly matches the tow vehicle, or you risk flipping on the highway. Because many of you will say that you or your friends have traveled for years without an accident, you may consider this a hard statement — but I see the accident results. If we expect to motivate trailer users to educate themselves, we must acknowledge that towing a trailer coach is a high-risk adventure. We cannot simply hide our heads in the sand and cry over the disasters. It doesn't work that way. Trailering can be made reasonably safe with the proper trailer, towing vehicle, hitching device, and knowledge. If you leave one of these out, you are living dangerously.

Fold-downs and telescoping trailers may be the safest for SUV owners.

These low-profile trailers may be an answer for many who tow with small vehicles. By lowering the height of the front and sides, you save money through increased efficiency and reduce the propensity for sway. Because of the recent emphasis on fuel-efficient vehicles, the size of vehicles has been reduced in proportion to power. Thus, the modern vehicle can have lots of power with less mass. Less mass means less weight, which means less control of a towed vehicle. If you plan to pull with a small truck, sedan, or SUV, you should seriously consider a high-quality, well-engineered telescoping trailer that matches the vehicle.

Safety problems with trailer coaches are split between poor engineering and bad hitching.

We have had some major balance problems with the engineering of trailer coaches — especially fold-downs. Balance isn't complicated, but it does take some thought. For example, the chart on the next page shows the design factors that make a trailer coach safe to tow. We know that too light hitch weights are very dangerous, and too heavy hitch weights can also be dangerous. Although these are trailering facts — not theories — many trailer engineers are often ignorant of their importance. You must, therefore, protect yourself and your family by not trusting the trailer builder.

We can only assume that the trailer you are considering is well designed with axles placed at least 70% back-of-ball-to-length ratio (which we call BOB ratio).

We can only assume that the trailer you are considering is well designed with axles placed at least 70% back-of-ball-to-length ratio (which we call BOB ratio). It should also have a

Design factors that make a trailer coach safe to tow are:

1. **A constant hitch weight between 10% and 12% of the total weight.**

2. **Axle placement at a back-of-ball-to-length ratio of at least 70%.**

3. **A minimum of 15% of the GVWR available for personal payload.**

That's all folks!

hitch weight right at 10% of the UVW and stay between 10% and 12% when loaded *because* the fresh water tank is over or slightly forward of the axles and the waste water tanks are in proximity of the axles. And, if properly designed, it will have a sufficient GVWR to carry at least 15% of the GVWR as personal payload. If the manufacturer's design is within these specifications, all you have to do is be sure you have an adequate tow vehicle and proper hitching methods.

Standard hitching devices are not always the way to go.

Most dealers will tell you that the best thing you can do to tow well is to install a weight-distributing hitch and a sway bar. Some will tell you that you don't need a sway bar if the hitch has one built-in. They won't tell you that sway bars are helpful in some situations and harmful in others. They won't tell you that hitching correctly is complicated. Most will charge you about $500 to install the hitch assembly, demonstrate how to put the hitch onto the tow vehicle, show you how to put on the spring bars, tell you how many links to drop if it has a chain adjustment (or how much to tighten if it has a screw adjustment), and as they wave good-bye they'll give you that crazy smile that tells you everything is all right. What the dealer tells you may be right, but chances are there's too much wrong. I know it's often wrong because I read the accident stories where, most of the time, the driver thought everything was as perfect as could be.

If you have an SUV and need to pull a trailer coach, there are alternatives.

SUV's up to 120 inches of wheelbase when combined with trailer coaches 20 feet in length or longer make the most dangerous RV combinations. Trailer coaches are absolutely unforgiving of any bad design, bad balance, heavy or light hitch weight, maladjusted hitching mechanisms, road-air movement, or adverse road conditions. If you are convinced that you need to pull a trailer coach that is longer than 20 feet with your SUV, such as that shown here, you need to think of a hitching device that will allow the trailer to move without wobbling the towing vehicle. Because hitching is a very comprehensive subject in itself, I recommend that you consult RV Consumer Group's CD guide *How to Tow Safely.*

Wheelbase needs to be understood.

If the wheelbase of the towing vehicle is too short, control can be lost in a matter of seconds. Many accidents with trailer coaches occur because the wheelbase of the towing vehicle is much too short for the weight and size of the trailer. Some describe it as the tail wagging the dog. Even though there are many warnings on this subject, many RV salespeople are still telling trailer buyers that their tow vehicle can pull anything on the lot. "Pull" may be partially true, but "control" may be way off. There is no question that insufficient wheelbase and lack of traction cause the majority of trailer coach accidents. This lack of control is compounded by poor design of the trailer relating to balance.

The photo at the top of the next page shows a truck and trailer combination that flipped with fatal results while traveling at normal highway speed. It's clear that the truck's wheelbase is not the problem. Now look at the trailer's back-of-ball-to-length ratio. The axles appear to be almost in the center of

the trailer. Also notice that there's no canopy on the truck — which indicates the bed was probably empty. By simple deduction, it's clear that the reason for the accident was probably a combination of bad trailer design and poor hitching. Wheelbase won't cover all sins, but a good wheelbase must be the first commandment of towing.

Although there is no short course on trailer towing, there are common sense rules you can follow. If the length of the trailer coach being towed with a conventional fixed-ball hitch is over two times the wheelbase of the towing vehicle, you are probably living dangerously. (With fifth wheels, you can go as much as three times the wheelbase.) RV Consumer Group has a formula that goes like this: The maximum towing length of a travel trailer coach begins at 20 feet for 110 inches of wheelbase of the towing vehicle. For each additional foot of trailer length, add 4 inches of wheelbase. Whichever one of these you use, remember one thing: Hitching equipment and techniques must be perfect if you want to be as safe as possible.

Before I leave this short bit of instruction on trailer coach towing, I want to warn you about fixed weight-distributing hitches. Whether they are weight-distributing hitches and whether they have sway bars does not alter what I am going to say. From all the accidents I have studied, I have concluded that trailer hitches with a solid connection between the towing vehicle and the towed vehicle are generally unsafe and should be considered archaic and obsolete.

I now warn you that this is a controversial subject that will raise hell among the many manufacturers of weight-distributing hitches and accessories. They will say that these hitches are good, provided that they are correctly used to pull a well-balanced trailer. That is the weakness of their argument. What they are saying, in essence, is that their hitches are unforgiving of trailer design and incorrect application of the hitch-tension devices. This unforgiving characteristic of fixed weight-distributing hitches causes thousands of accidents every year. If you have another explanation for the great number of accidents involving trailer coaches, RVCG invites your response — send your email to rvgroup@rv.org.

Fifth wheel travel trailers are very forgiving and generally safe.

Fifth wheels make wonderful homes on wheels. I have literally talked to thousands of fulltimers and have found that those who are pulling fifth wheels are the happiest RVers. They are happy because the "rig" is practical and forgiving. They can get into fifth-wheel fulltiming with almost any budget. They always have their miniature home and a "get-around" vehicle. They find that maintenance on both vehicles is no more extensive than on a fixed dwelling and a family car.

Most RVers find fifth wheels are safe provided that the trailer is reasonably balanced and not over-loaded. If they travel level with wheels and brakes operating correctly, they feel comfortable about towing under almost any highway condition. On the right is a photo of a fifth wheel that is obviously not running level. Notice that most of the trailer weight is on the rear axle. This will not only wear the suspension components extensively, but it will diminish braking and control. When trailer axles are in tandem, it is extremely important that the weight of the total load be distributed evenly among all axle assemblies.

Another safety problem occurs when the total of the fifth wheel's weight and the towing vehicle's weight exceeds the gross combined weight rating (GCWR) of the truck. When this happens, RVers are quick to admit that they allow themselves to get into the "roller-coaster effect" — which means they make up speed on the downgrade because they are underpowered on the upgrade. Fast speeds on the downgrades can be dangerous to life, limb, and nerves. Stories of "white knuckles" in such scenarios are common. Like with all RVs, it's important that fifth-wheel travelers abide by common sense rules of not overloading either truck or trailer. If the trailer/truck combination is anywhere near the maximum gross combined weight rating of the truck, you must have an exhaust or jake brake. Although fifth wheels are forgiving of driver errors, they are not fail-safe.

The ever-present problem of occupants sleeping with propane heating devices that are poorly ventilated is still causing many deaths among RVers.

Slide-in campers are unsafe when they're unstable.

Because passengers don't ride in a slide-in (it's often illegal but should never be done anyway), safety for the occupants is built into the pickup. Safety with slide-ins usually involves three issues: 1) instability, 2) stopping, and 3) sleeping death. Instability is the number one reason for unhappy slide-in camper owners. Because many truck campers overload the truck chassis, the inability to stop in an emergency is the cause of many accidents. And, the ever-present problem of occupants sleeping with propane heating devices that are poorly ventilated is still causing many deaths among RVers. All of these potential safety hazards can easily be avoided by conscientious adherence to basic rules.

Stopping and pulling power are too often ignored by slide-in camper users.

Every pickup is designed to carry a specific weight within the bed. "In the bed," means below the profile of the cab. Thus a one-half-ton pickup may carry up to 1,500 pounds if the entire load is below the profile of the cab. The suspension is not designed to carry a load with a center of mass above the bed sides — which could be loaded to the height of the cab. Most three-quarter-ton pickups can effectively carry between

2,000 and 2,500 pounds in the bed, but most do not work well with a 2,500-pound camper with most of the weight above the sides of the bed. A one-ton pickup seems to work well with a load of firewood weighing between 3,000 and 3,500 pounds (3,500 for duals), but a 3,000-pound slide-in on the same truck can make a very unstable RV. This limitation needs to be considered before you jump into the purchase of a slide-in camper.

You need to consider pulling power with slide-ins as much as you would with motor homes. The pulling power is specified in the manufacturer's trailer guide as gross combined weight rating (GCWR). This is the maximum you should pull with a specific engine and gear train (transmission and rear axle). The one thing you must impress into your mind is that the GCWR is pulling power — not stopping power. Stopping power is determined by the gross vehicle weight rating (GVWR) of the pickup. The difference is extremely important. If you exceed the GVWR with a non-braked load, you will not stop within the specific distance required for that particular vehicle. Because a slide-in camper has no brakes, it must figure into both the GVWR and the GCWR. If, in addition, you pull any vehicle without brakes, it must also be figured into both the GVWR and GCWR. However, if the boat trailer, horse trailer, or auto you are towing is equipped with its own stopping power, it needs to be figured only into the GCWR. Because RV salespeople are generally not well informed about your truck's capacity, you must get this information on your own. You will also need to have a very good idea of what the loaded slide-in will weigh as it sits on the pickup.

My rules for matching slide-in campers to pickup trucks are simple, albeit somewhat conservative.

A half-ton pickup shouldn't carry any slide-in camper that extends above the cab or beyond the bed. This pretty much limits the half-ton to a pop-up slide-in specifically designed

> *The one thing you must impress into your mind is that the GCWR is pulling power — not stopping power.*

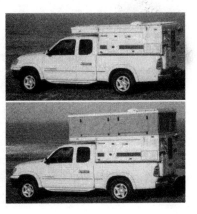

for half-ton trucks. If you want to put a slide-in on a half-ton, you must adhere to the bed-load specifications from the truck's manufacturer. It is important that you do not exceed the gross axle weight rating for the rear axle or the truck's gross vehicle weight rating (GVWR). Because a half-ton pickup is designed for family utility use, the suspension is light and soft. Any overloading will mean some difficulty in steering and stopping. Although I've seen half-ton pickups with 9-foot slide-in campers, driving such a combination is more foolish than brave.

A 3/4-ton pickup will generally handle a slide-in that extends to one foot beyond the bed — although I prefer no more than a half-foot beyond the bed. This extra length allows extra room for a bathroom and holding tank. If the slide-in's center of gravity is designed for an 8-foot bed, this should allow for reasonable balance. You should always be certain that the weight of the slide-in — including supplies and personal gear — does not exceed 85% of the pickup's bed capacity.

A one-ton with dual wheels is the only pickup that will work for slide-ins that exceed the bed by 12 inches or more. If

the slide-in is particularly light — say, between 2,500 and 3,000 pounds when loaded with water and supplies — performance should be acceptable with single rear wheels. If the floor of the slide-in exceeds 9 feet, I am adamant that the only safe pickup must have dual wheels on the back. You should also understand that no pickup is designed to carry a slide-in longer than 9 feet — which typically weighs over 3,000 pounds loaded.

When I was on a photo-fishing expedition, I came across the two truck campers shown to the left. The top photo shows a slide-in that fits into the bed. Notice that the truck has a long wheelbase because it has an extended cab. There should be no handling problems with this setup. In the lower photo, however, notice two things: One, the slide-in extends about a foot beyond the bed of the truck, and two, the boat trailer probably has a tongue weight of at least 500 pounds. On a light-duty truck that is not suspended and hitched properly, there could easily be too little weight on the front wheels for highway safety. This setup could create steering problems.

Rock 'n Rolling is typical slide-in behavior.

Although trucks may be designated as "camper specials", they are still designed to carry a payload on the bed. Any extension beyond the bed will encourage the truck to "rock" under some road conditions — something the truck is not designed to handle. The longer the extension, the worse the rocking. When you consider that the typical slide-in has a center of mass well above the truck bed that contributes to roll from side-to-side, and an extension beyond the bed that contributes to rocking, you can see why many campers go down the road rocking and rolling. Because many slide-in campers are poorly engineered for side-to-side balance, you might begin to understand why a poorly balanced slide-in with a tendency to rock and roll might be a safety hazard on a highway that's rough and heavily trafficked with large cargo trucks. A slide-in truck camper can be an economical, safe, and practical way of RVing, but if you want to do it right, be sure to match the slide-in to the truck.

What about slideout rooms?

Slideout rooms for travel trailers were introduced in the mid 1980's as a replacement for the tip-out room — which was operated manually. They became extremely popular in the early 1990's and, not much later, started showing up in motor homes. They actually worked as a benefit in fifth wheels and trailer coaches because the capacity of these RVs was practically unlimited (i.e., by adding axles). Even though I saw lots of problems with the first slideouts, most deficiencies had to

do with reliability and durability. By the mid 1990's, however, most engineering problems with slideouts were behind us.

With motor homes, the slideout room is a safety issue. An obvious safety problem has to do with the extra weight of the slideout room — which is usually between 500 and 800 pounds. With overweight already a major issue, the slideout room became a battle of consumer demands for more space entering an already existing conflict about needing higher capacity chassis. Although there has been a bit of resolution with the advent of new and upgraded chassis, the overload issue is still with us.

As you probably know, to install a slideout room a manufacturer has to leave a large hole in the sidewall. This means that the built-in structural strength is simply not there — thus, structural integrity is compromised. We already know that many motor homes will not sustain a rollover without the walls collapsing or falling off. The big question now being asked in regard to rollovers is whether an otherwise sound motor home would collapse because of the reduced wall structure. With some brands, I believe it will.

The popularity of slideout rooms has made it very difficult for me to push for restraints. As you can see from the pictures on these pages, slideouts are indeed extremely popular with manufacturers and RVers. For trailers and slide-in truck campers, it is simply an issue of weight and balance — something that can be resolved with good engineering. However, with motor homes I firmly believe that the safety issue will get worse before it gets better. If you are seriously considering any type of motor home, I urge you to consider one that does not have a slideout room.

Conclusion: Walk easy.

Selecting the right RV is a time-consuming and expensive experience. It's time-consuming because your opinion will change constantly and conjectures will become common. It's expensive because you'll most likely go beyond your budget to adjust to every new desire that surfaces.

Selecting an RV is a challenge because it taxes your energy and emotions to dangerous limits. You will be exhilarated one moment and plunged into depression the next. You will often be so frustrated and tired that you'll be ready to accept the next salesperson as your rescuer. Trash begins to look good. Defects are easy to excuse. Statements seem more truthful. Money is no longer an issue. If you aren't careful, you will buy something that you don't want or need.

But you're not going to let this happen because you're going to select the right RV by inspecting it carefully and following the ten rules for buying in section 3 of this volume. You'll use common sense, even when you're tired and frustrated. You'll keep your objectives in the forefront and not allow a beguiling salesperson to sway you. You're going to exercise determination. You're going to buy the right RV for the right price. You're going to walk easy. You're going to have fun.

Section 2

How to Inspect

Introduction to Walkabout

What we've learned about RV building tells us we must exercise scrutiny. It tells us this for good reasons. An RV is not an automobile. It is not built by a combination of robots and union members. It is primarily built by low-paid men and women who have learned their trade by training with other low-paid workers. In some states, particularly Indiana where most of the factories are located, workers drift from factory to factory. In many cases, they learn RV design by visiting various factories to see how it's done. More often than not a floor plan is used because another manufacturer is using it successfully — whether it is correctly designed or not. Too often quality control depends on the profit rather than being an essential ingredient of the budget. If you want to be critical, the picture can be pretty bleak.

But it's not all as bad as it looks. The demands RV consumers have made from RV manufacturers have kept about half of these manufacturers from building crackerboxes. I think this is about as good as it's going to get — at least for a while. In the meantime, we need to work with the half that is trying to build good RVs in spite of the many problems that exist in their industry. This good half has a conscience. They work hard at designing quality into their vehicles. They try hard to hire workers who have a desire to build a good product. They work at quality control, and when they make a mistake they take care of buyers' complaints. I really believe this good half of RV builders has heart.

Unlike an automobile, every RV needs a complete inspection by the buyer. One new car in a giant sales lot of hundreds is pretty much like another. Although there may be some differences in colors and optional equipment, the workmanship, materials, and design will be almost identical. An RV is not like this. Every brand, every model, and every vehicle is different. Because every vehicle is different in many ways you, the buyer, must carefully inspect every RV you are considering for its features and quality of construction. For many, this is an unnerving prospect. But it's really not as hard as you may think at first. If you consider the size of investment you are making for an unnecessary product, you psych yourself into working harder. As you look more, you will see more. As you see more, you will see more clearly. As you see more clearly, you will begin to make better decisions. It's not just the money you're trying to save, it's the quality of life you're trying to achieve with your RV.

As hard as I am on the RV industry for their haphazard methods, like me, you're going to be very surprised how much unexpected quality you are going to find as you get better at looking for details. You will be pleased to discover features that are totally unexpected nuggets of gold. You'll begin to find that some manufacturers don't hesitate to do small things below the surface that add to the durability or usability of the RV. You'll gradually become more positive than negative. As you start smiling more (when the seller can't see you), you'll start enjoying your search.

If you believe what I have just told you, you'll agree that a walkabout is totally necessary. You can't get by without a complete inspection if you want the best you can get for your money. Whether you buy used or new, even if you order from the factory, you'll need to do a complete walkabout before you accept an RV. It would be foolhardy not to do so.

A walkabout will reveal the good and bad of the workmanship, materials, and design of things you can see. From what you see you can only assume that similar conditions exist beneath the skin. However, this is not always true. I have seen RVs that look good on the surface but have terrible workmanship, materials, and design in the structure. Because this does not happen with well-rated manufacturers (see the *RV Ratings Guide CD*), by choosing brands that have a history of good performance you should feel comfortable that "what you see is what you get."

A walkabout is a combination of a walk-around and a walk-through. The walk-around is an inspection of the exterior and the walk-through is an inspection of the interior. Some buyers do a walk-around first and then if it passes inspection they'll do a walk-through. Some are more interested in floor plans, so they do a walk-through first and then a walk-around if they are still interested. Either way will work provided your eyes remain open.

In this book, we're going to do a complete walkabout to show you features from a composite of dozens of RVs — both new and used. To make it more exciting (and keep you awake) I'll mix types. Because RV features are much the same regardless of type, I don't think this will be disconcerting. You won't be able to touch and smell as if you're in a real RV, but I think you'll get the idea.

To make the sequence easy to remember, we'll do it in 10 easy steps. It all started with Roy Easton, a friend and volunteer who began with me in this process during 1987. We developed these 10 steps and found that they work well for both neophyte buyers and experienced appraisers. The 10 steps are:

1) profile
2) skin
3) roof
4) structure
5) chassis
6) galley
7) bathroom
8) woodwork
9) lining
10) fixtures

You'll notice that 1 through 5 are walk-around steps (exterior) and 6 through 10 are walk-through steps (interior). The distinction is necessary because some people are good at walk-arounds and some are good at walk-throughs. When couples work together on a walkabout, it is often practical to let one partner make a quick walk-around and the other do a quick walk-through. If the model is then placed on the worth-considering list, a complete walkabout should be made with both partners discussing each item. As you do each part of the walkabout (the walk-around and the walk-through), you must concentrate on all five steps of that part. Keep notes on each step as you move through each part.

A walkabout is designed to be revealing. It should reveal the negatives and the positives. It is important that you understand that we are going to be primarily looking for negatives. Because much will always be right about every RV model you look at (the salespeople will point out those features to you), you must look for the things that are wrong. If too much is wrong, you will be an unhappy camper. You will undoubtedly need to make some compromises, but *you* must make those decisions — not the salesperson.

So, let's do a walkabout.

Step 1 — Profile

If you are a new RVer, always begin by asking yourself some basic questions while studying the profile. The most important question you can ask yourself is, "Will it work for what I want it to do?" As I mentioned previously, this question is important because if the RV is the wrong type or size, you won't be satisfied and you'll trade it before it's earned its way. Unless you can afford to make a financial mistake, take time to study the profile with a critical eye.

If you are already an RVer but want to move on to something different, you still need to think just as carefully about whether you will buy new or used. I have found that as many bad choices have been made by "experienced" RVers because they were sure that they knew exactly what they wanted. In the end, it didn't turn out that way. They tell me that they got caught up into moving too fast for many reasons. Regardless of the reasons, they now wish they had slowed down.

Buying used can save you money by the basketful if you do it right. Doing it right means looking right. To look right you have to look with open eyes and open mind. You need to see things that will easily get by you if you aren't concentrating. For buying used, it is important to have a checklist. It won't guarantee success, but it reduces the risk of making a big mistake.

When you make a habit of reflecting on the entire RV from a distance, you'll know that you have acquired a new philosophy of buying. You'll know that your focus will be different when you look at it up close. After a few times you'll look at every RV from a distance, from close up, and from recall. That's right — "Recall." Once you get in the habit of reflecting from a distance and focusing close up, your memory will retain some important things to help you make comparisons. Let's begin Step 1 with our "reflect, focus, and recall" philosophy.

Some things to ponder:

Although the class A is extremely popular with prospective buyers, there are some who are uncomfortable with its inherent characteristics — primarily its boxy shape and the lack of a frontal crush area. Because of its ability to catch wind and air from passing trucks, short wheelbase class A's are particularly subject to difficulties in handling. With the large frontal area constantly pushing air, the wear and tear on the engine is high while the fuel efficiency is low.

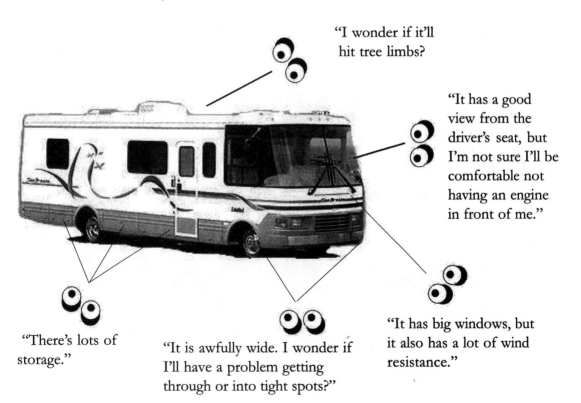

"I wonder if it'll hit tree limbs?

"It has a good view from the driver's seat, but I'm not sure I'll be comfortable not having an engine in front of me."

"There's lots of storage."

"It is awfully wide. I wonder if I'll have a problem getting through or into tight spots?"

"It has big windows, but it also has a lot of wind resistance."

Some things to ponder:

Manufacturers of low-profile class A's have been trying to gain acceptance for over 20 years. Although growth has been slow, and sometimes absent, I think its time has come. A major stumbling block has been the cost of production, which is higher than for the standard class A per square foot. There are some good low-profiles on the used market at very attractive prices. However, as of this writing, they are becoming more rare.

"I like the low profile because it will be easy to get under things."

It's wider than a van, but it drives like a small truck."

"Hmm. I can't see any outside storage. Where will I store things?"

"There's a lot of protection in the front. It even has a solid bumper."

Some things to ponder:

The class B is undoubtedly the best motor home for use as a runabout. It will get into almost any parking space a family car can. It is not a compact, but neither is it considered large by American standards. It is, however, an RV in that it has basic living amenities. If you need to go for a day, a weekend, or a week, the class B can work perfectly. It is quite fuel efficient and versatile. It is very practical for active seniors who want to keep a home while having away-from-home adventures.

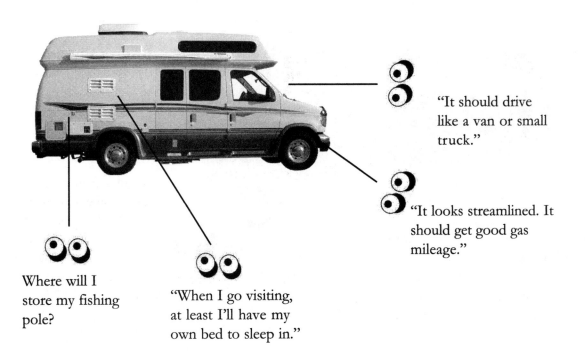

"It should drive like a van or small truck."

"It looks streamlined. It should get good gas mileage."

Where will I store my fishing pole?

"When I go visiting, at least I'll have my own bed to sleep in."

Some things to ponder:

The class C (mini) has been the number-one choice of RVing families for decades. If the structural integrity is good, it should be safe for those passengers in the cockpit and those seated inside the house. It usually has plenty of storage, and longer ones might even have a slideout room. However, the class C is limited by chassis capacity, leaving those in the 30-foot range subject to overweight and out-of-balance characteristics.

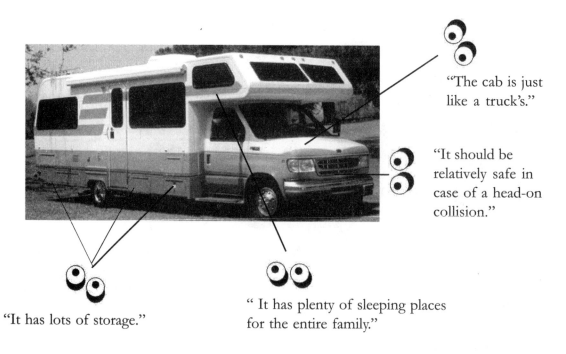

"The cab is just like a truck's."

"It should be relatively safe in case of a head-on collision."

"It has lots of storage."

" It has plenty of sleeping places for the entire family."

Some things to ponder:

The low-profile class C is often mistaken for a class B; but because it's built on a cutaway chassis, it is a class C. Because of its streamlined body style, it should handle well when built with a good wheelbase. Because it is usually more expensive than a standard class C, it has not gained popularity — but I believe its time is coming.

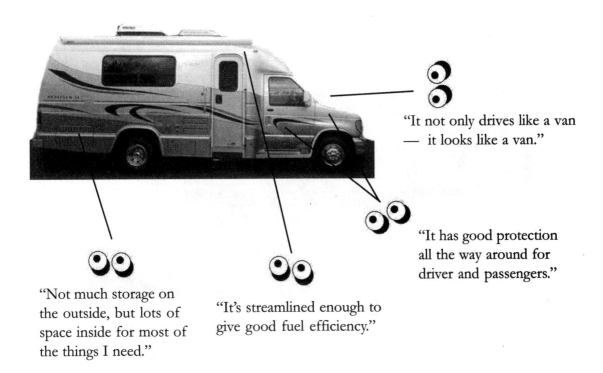

"It not only drives like a van — it looks like a van."

"It has good protection all the way around for driver and passengers."

"Not much storage on the outside, but lots of space inside for most of the things I need."

"It's streamlined enough to give good fuel efficiency."

Some things to ponder:

Since a class C+ can be as small as a standard class C or as large as the longest class A, it allows you a multitude of choices. You can buy from a line-production manufacturer or from one of many smaller custom builders. If you go custom, you can pretty much choose the chassis and the floor plan.

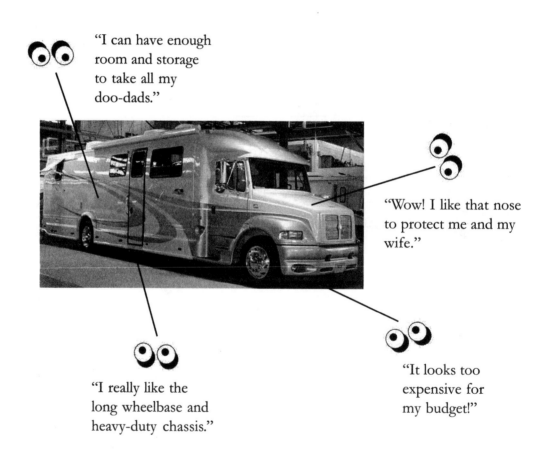

"I can have enough room and storage to take all my doo-dads."

"Wow! I like that nose to protect me and my wife."

"I really like the long wheelbase and heavy-duty chassis."

"It looks too expensive for my budget!"

Some things to ponder:

More trailer coaches have been sold during the last 50 years than any other type of RV. I started with one in 1956 and I still have one. They are versatile in use and in towing because they can be towed behind a sedan, a van, or a truck. They are available in a wide variety of sizes, and come with a good selection of floor plans. Their only drawback is a sensitivity to hitching. If you don't hitch it right, a trailer coach will turn on you — literally!

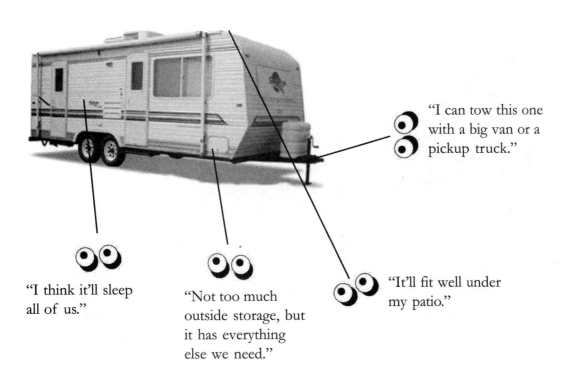

"I can tow this one with a big van or a pickup truck."

"I think it'll sleep all of us."

"Not too much outside storage, but it has everything else we need."

"It'll fit well under my patio."

Some things to ponder:

Some trailer coaches are made for fulltiming. These RVs are made with high-quality design, materials, and workmanship to suit full-time living. They are in every way a travel home. They have the best of RV equipment because it's needed for fulltiming. Trailer coaches designed for fulltiming should be comfortable in almost any kind of weather. I always recommend these RVs for those who are serious about becoming snowbirds — as well as fulltiming.

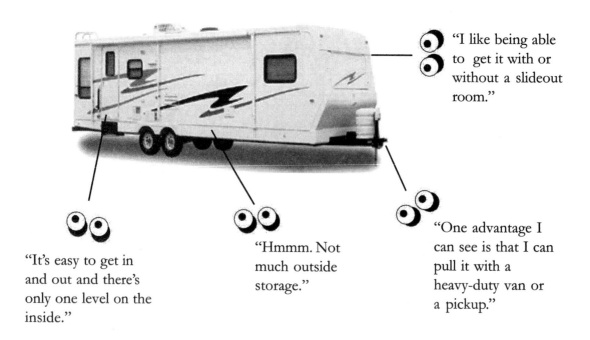

"I like being able to get it with or without a slideout room."

"It's easy to get in and out and there's only one level on the inside."

"Hmmm. Not much outside storage."

"One advantage I can see is that I can pull it with a heavy-duty van or a pickup."

Some things to ponder:

The fifth wheel has great trailering characteristics. It also has a good variety of floor plans and sizes. Fifth wheels up to 30 feet long are most popular with families for vacationing and with retired people for snowbirding. Behind the right truck, the fifth wheel is a pleasure to tow for most people. With all this said, you must keep in mind that a fifth wheel is not fail-safe.

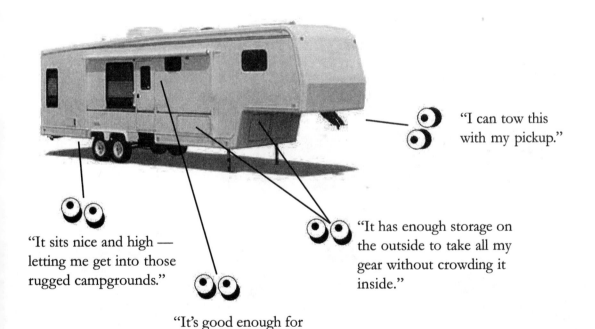

"I can tow this with my pickup."

"It sits nice and high — letting me get into those rugged campgrounds."

"It has enough storage on the outside to take all my gear without crowding it inside."

"It's good enough for vacations or to take south for the winter."

Some things to ponder:

Fifth wheels designed for fulltiming are usually big RVs. If they have three axles, or tandems with duals, you know you shouldn't tow them with a pickup truck. Because they are designed with structure and equipment that will satisfy full-time living, they are usually heavy. The RV doesn't have to be big to give it fulltiming quality. RVCG has listed a few manufacturers who build fulltiming fifth wheels that can be towed with pickups.

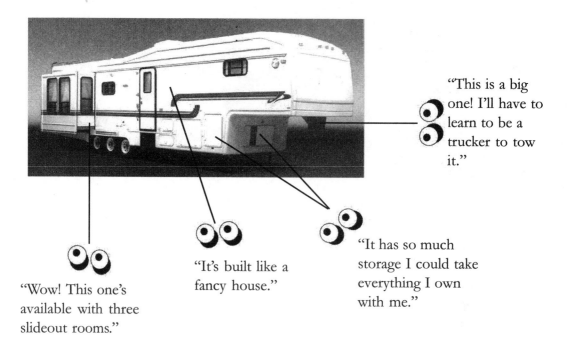

"This is a big one! I'll have to learn to be a trucker to tow it."

"Wow! This one's available with three slideout rooms."

"It's built like a fancy house."

"It has so much storage I could take everything I own with me."

Some things to ponder:

Designed specifically for families and sports enthusiasts, the toy hauler is exactly what the name implies. The large cargo room in the rear has a ramp that also serves as a door and wall — enabling you to take your bicycles, motorcycles, or ATVs into the desert, forest, or boondocks. Although toy haulers are available in motor homes (SURV), they are most common as trailer coaches and fifth wheels (SUT).

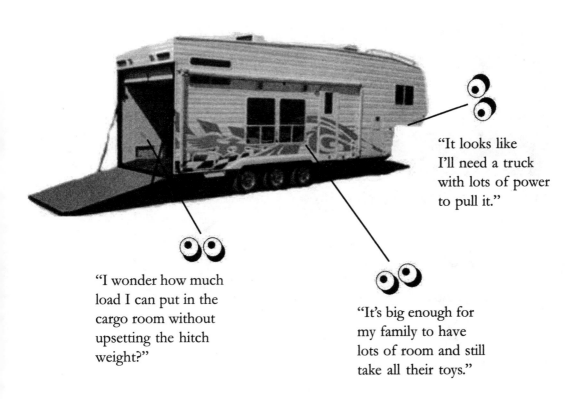

"It looks like I'll need a truck with lots of power to pull it."

"I wonder how much load I can put in the cargo room without upsetting the hitch weight?"

"It's big enough for my family to have lots of room and still take all their toys."

Some things to ponder:

The concept of the expandable trailer came along with the popularity of SUV's. It's actually a trailer coach with slideout beds. Although the concept is good, I'm not sure that they will be as durable as one might think at first. There's a lot of canvas, mechanism, and lightweight building techniques. Water leakage at the front hatch has been a problem.

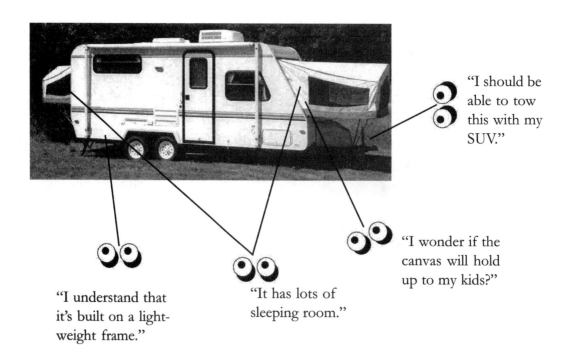

"I should be able to tow this with my SUV."

"I wonder if the canvas will hold up to my kids?"

"I understand that it's built on a lightweight frame."

"It has lots of sleeping room."

Some things to ponder:

A fold-down trailer is ideal for the many families who have a light-weight vehicle and want a portable camp. Although there are some negatives, it has served RVing families for over three decades. Fold-downs in the 1,000-pound range rarely give any problems; but when they climb above 2,000 pounds there are often serious problems with towing.

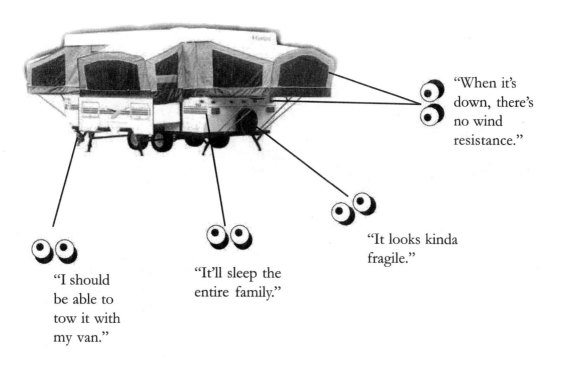

"When it's down, there's no wind resistance."

"It looks kinda fragile."

"It'll sleep the entire family."

"I should be able to tow it with my van."

Some things to ponder:

A slide-in camper can be the right RV for the right person. It is not for everyone. It is ideal for someone who has a truck and wants to carry a small home on its back. When done correctly, a slide-in can work well in conjunction with a boat and trailer or a horse trailer. As I mentioned previously, you need to give careful thought to this kind of purchase. A truck plus camper can cost as much as a good class C motor home.

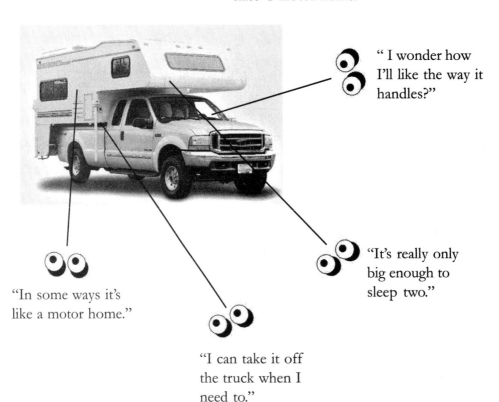

" I wonder how I'll like the way it handles?"

"It's really only big enough to sleep two."

"In some ways it's like a motor home."

"I can take it off the truck when I need to."

Step 2 — Skin

We've always heard about things being "skin deep." Although it implies that skin may be appealing, don't ignore what's under it. We can go on and on about beauty versus utility, but let's face it— most of us want some of both. Like the walls of a home, the outer surface of an RV must look good while keeping you comfortable and secure.

When doing a walkabout, I consider the skin to be whatever can be seen and touched from the outside. This means the siding, front cap, rear cap, roof covering, doors, windows, storage-compartment doors, and slideout rooms. Like other parts of the walkabout, there will be some overlap. For example, you can't study the storage compartments without seeing some of the structure. If you're looking at the siding and see signs of delamination, you begin to look more closely around the roof edges to see if there are signs of water leaks; and you might even want to open the brochure and see how the sidewalls are structured. You might even take the time now to move right into studying the structure to see if it is indeed a laminated sidewall.

The walkabout is nothing more than a 10-step mental and paper check. This is your assurance that you won't miss something important. In some cases, you might check items in 3 or 4 steps at one stop. Checking out the skin is but one step.

One note of caution: This book cannot cover every type of skin or every way that skin is attached to the structure.

Good front caps look good and are water repellent.

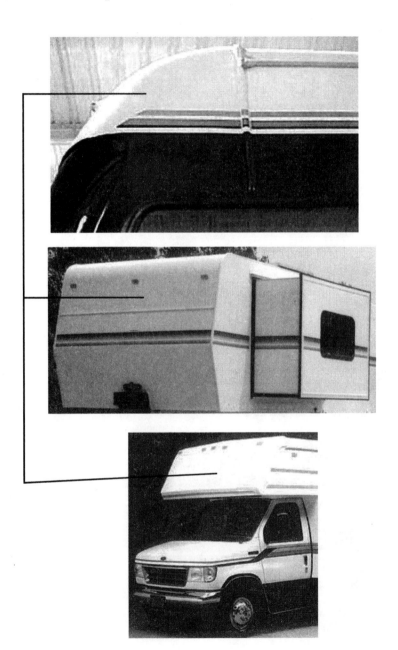

When you are driving down the highway at 60 miles per hour into rain with head-winds of 20 miles-per-hour, water is hitting the RV at 80 miles-per-hour. The front cap should be designed to repell water at this velocity.

A poorly-designed cap usually lasts about 5 years.

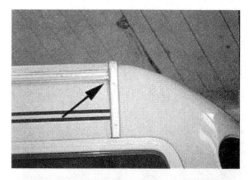

The front cap shown here is lower than the roof. This means that down the road there is a good chance that rain water will leak into the interior.

This roof looks good at first, but notice that the roof and the front cap appear to abut. The trim and sealant are all that stop water leaks.

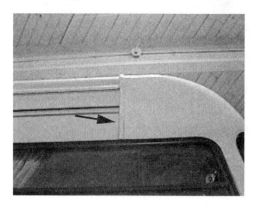

Although this front cap is well over the roof, the sides are not snug to the sidewall. Any leaks in this area could cause delamination.

Although the workmanship on this motor home looks so good I wouldn't expect it to leak during the first 5 years of its life, what about 10 to 15 years down the road? Can you now see the design deficiency?

This motor home has a cap that extends well over the roof, but the sidewall protection is skimpy at best.

Because motor homes work hard, design must compensate for movement.

It has been proven that bad corners like this one give problems when the motor home has been around for a while. Roof-to-cap joints need to be forgiving to body twist.

We know this roof is leaking because there are water stains on the ceiling and interior walls. Apparently the design does not compensate for body twisting. Water hitting forward-facing seams is bound to find entrance sooner or later if careful attention-to-detail is not given during manufacture and maintenance.

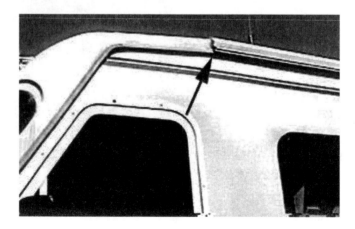

Leaks at the cap mean destruction of the sidewalls.

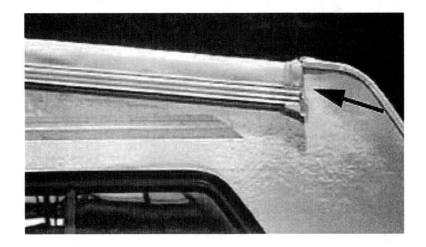

These two roofs have not protected the sidewalls.
Close inspection shows the beginning of deterioration.

It's a fact: If the skin is glued to the wall structure, it can delaminate.

You need to get into the habit of pushing on the walls to see if you feel any 'give', bump, or waviness. Like kicking tires, this exercise will keep you focused on the subject.

This wall is tight, flat, and straight. If it were not glued (laminated), it could feel bulgy when the sun heats it and look like a pregnant cow. It's okay for a loose-fitting (aluminum) skin to expand, but not for other types.

Even skin that has the "ribbed" effect, as shown here, can delaminate. Actually, because this skin does not allow as much inside surface to contact the wall structure, the lamination process is more critical.

Slideout seals vary greatly in effectiveness.

Slideouts need to sit straight and flush with the structure. If they are crooked in any way, there will be trouble down the road.

Be sure there's no way for light, moisture, or dirt to get through the seals. Leakage of these elements is a major complaint of slideout-room owners. Seals should be pliable but stiff enough to scrape the sides.

When you see a torn slideout seal on a brand-new RV, it makes you wonder what else is wrong. Torn seals mean that the manufacturer has chosen the wrong material or is using the wrong design.

Slideout trim is an indicator of the attention-to-detail given to the RV.

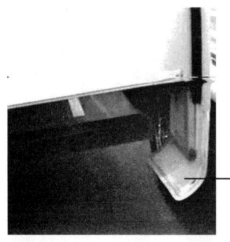

Slideout skirting should look like this one. It should have no jagged edges or protruding screws. When you grab it, it should be stiff.

The slideout skirting must never be jagged like this one. It has rough cuts and very sharp edges. You can even see a cut that looks like a mistake.

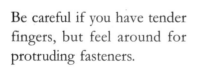

Be careful if you have tender fingers, but feel around for protruding fasteners.

Compartment doors and linings give RVers many gripes.

Because compartments are supposed to be secure from theft and water, there are many different designs. This design is most common for trailers and entry-level motor homes. I carefully check hinges and seals to predict failures.

This compartment door that lowers has some negatives, but leaking at the hinges is not one of them. Doors like this over 30 inches long need two latches but should have three.

This a common compartment and door configuration. The hinges need to be good and the seals capable of sealing. Notice that there is a protrusion to deflect water that gets past the hinges.

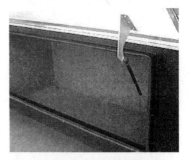

This compartment with tray looks good, but if it leaks the water stays in the tray. Thick fiberglass, good hinges, and multiple latches are extremely important to this design.

Although rear caps are mainly for looks, if not designed and installed correctly, water leaks are possible.

You need to notice where the rear cap overlaps the walls and roof. Sometimes the cap is too big and sealant is applied to fill the space. Inspect all corners closely.

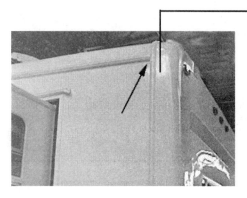 

Where there's a rear entrance and a rear cap, look closely for good reinforcements around doors and windows.

This is not a rear cap. It is a standard wall with radius trim to give the effect of a cap. It seems to work well if the trim is firm fiberglass and well sealed.

**Windows keep nature where *you* want it —
outside or inside.**

This is a good set of torque windows. Let the wind blow, the rain fall, and the dust fly — you're in control.

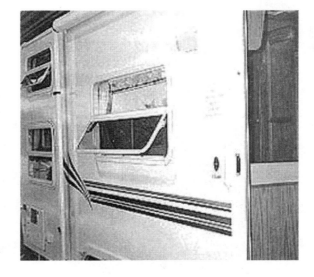

These small torque windows are excellent for galley or for bedroom.

Doors are more than a convenience.

Most doors have radius framing. The rounded effect helps prevent cracking of the walls at the doors, plus most RVers think it looks better. The three hinges are important to study for sturdiness, as is the workmanship attaching the door frame and the door itself.

This door has a high-quality piano hinge that looks sturdy. Be sure you always study the operation of the screen door — especially the latches. They are not always the same.

Square-cut doors have been common in the past but are now losing favor. We find that most deficiencies occur in the workmanship of building and installing these doors and frames. Jamming is a big problem with these doors when you really need them to open.

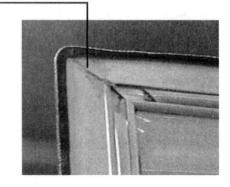

Step 3 — Structure

The construction of an RV, like that of a home, will determine the comfort and security of its future occupants. To find out how it's built during a walkabout is impossible. You cannot see inside the walls or between the roof covering and the ceiling. However, you can do something else.

Remember when you visited the doctor's office and were asked to open your mouth and say, "Aah?" The doctor can tell a lot about your general health by this simple procedure. Well, you can do something similar with an RV. By peering into storage compartments, you can get a good idea of the workmanship, materials, and design of the general structure.

It's critical to have an idea of how the four walls are put together in an RV. (Even on a motor home, you should consider that the front end is like a wall because it is protection against the elements.) RV walls are structured with wood, aluminum, or steel framing. Many have a combination of wood and metal. Some are structured like a wood-framed house where the skin is simply hung onto the studs, while others have laminated walls. (If you are not clear about the various structural techniques for walls, go back to chapter 3 and go through the factory tour again.) To keep your head clear, always do your homework on the structural requirements of RVs before you do a complete walkabout.

Getting the structure down so that you have an idea how it's built will probably require some research. I go to factories where I can see what kind of materials are used and how it's all put together. It also gives me a good idea of the capability of the RV to hold together for 20 years. At the factory, or during a walkabout, you can get a good idea of the philosophy of the management. If the joints are sloppily fit, it's because the management wants it that way. Believe me, they know how they build an RV. They know if they do good work, mediocre work, or bad work. Those people working with the manufacturing process know what they are doing, and they have a reason for doing it that way.

This chapter will introduce you to some ideas and methods for qualifying the structural integrity of the RV you are considering. If you decide to be aggressive in this step, you will find yourself consuming more time than you might have planned. You might have to go to another model of the same brand to get a better view of the internal structure. Sometimes I have to go through a number of models just to see if the structure is as it is claimed to be. I may have to climb into the forward compartment of one and a rear compartment of another. When I look through utility access doors, I always see something of value, so I never miss those "peekholes." Even though the completion of this one step may take you 10 to 20 minutes, it will be worth the time spent for many of you.

It won't tell all, but it tells a lot.

This one looks so clean and so tight it must be steel or aluminum structured — but it isn't. This compartment shows a class C motor home from a manufacturer who does top quality work with wood. Just climb on in and you'll see what it's made of and how it's put together.

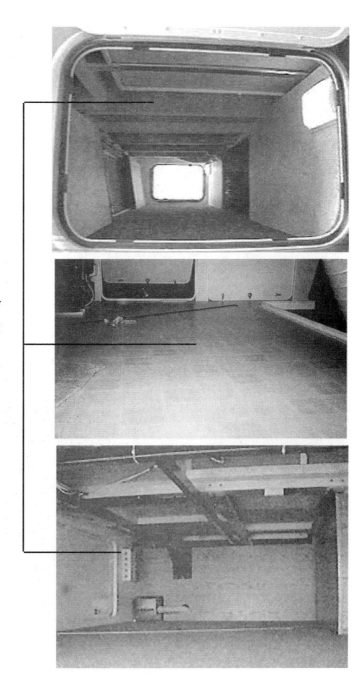

No, it is not the living room floor. It's the large front compartment of a fifth wheel. It has wood framing and there's enough room for you to lie inside comfortably to study the structure.

In this compartment, as with many, you'll get a chance to see some utilities. With this combination, if you study it carefully, you will definitely get a good idea of what's under the skin.

Look up, look down, look all around.

When you lie on your back, you're going to ask yourself some pretty interesting questions — like, "Why does this floor have both chipboard and plywood in its construction? I wonder which one they promote?"

You'll begin to wonder why they couldn't have changed some of the little things that would have made good sense — like using a dark sealant and applying it more smoothly. (Maybe they didn't plan on anyone climbing inside?)

Whether they're brand new or 10 years old, you're going to see some things that are not so pretty.

Some things will go beyond being indicators. You'll see things that should disgust you.
(This one was seen at a show.)

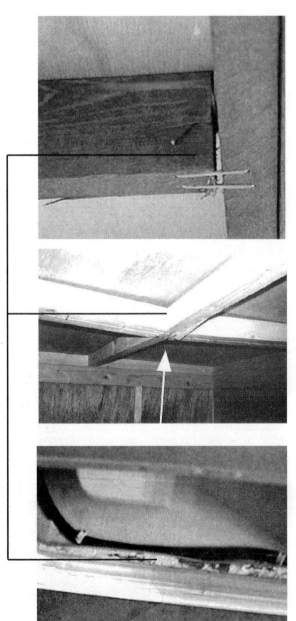

This one is just a few years old, but imagine someone who weighs 250 pounds stomping on this floor.

Look for things like this. You can see the panel separation and the foam insulation disintegrating before it's even been used.

You can see when they're good.

By crawling into the compartments, you can often see the floor structure and sometimes the wall structure. It's a great way to learn about building techniques.

Step 4 — Roof

As you do the walkabout, you'll probably find that gaining access to the roof can be a real bummer. If you're young and agile, you might just grab hold of that ladder, yank yourself up, and climb like hell. If you're just a bit closer to 100, like I am, you might want to have a couple of people on the ground to catch you in case you slip. Take the word of someone who's done it for 20-odd years — it's an adventure. Seriously, if you can get a look at the roof in a safe manner and with the permission of whomever, you might find it another indicator of what will befall the RV in the future.

I have found the roof is indeed a crystal ball when it comes to longevity. By looking at the roof, I can get a general idea of the kind of trouble the structure is going to have in the next ten years. It's not mysterious or magical. It's a simple skill acquired from climbing thousands of ladders to look at roofs and studying thousands of complaints relating to leaking roofs. How well I remember shocking the industry when I lambasted the one-piece thin aluminum roof that was used so heavily in the 1980's. It was a terrible roof because it worked so hard at twisting, shrinking, expanding, and rattling that it was almost impossible for it to stop seeping water. Of course, most of the time, problems arose a few years after the warranty had elapsed. Although this thin one-piece aluminum roof is pretty much gone, roof problems are still with us. It's one of those problems that the RV industry has allowed to go on and on because the damage usually occurs 3 to 5 years down the road. When they don't have to pay for it, they don't worry about fixing it.

Special Note: Do not confuse the thin one-piece aluminum roof with the heavy-gauge supported aluminun roof built by Lazy Daze, a small class C motor home manufacturer. Their roof has proven to be superb.

So if you get can get on the roof for an inspection, do it. If you can't, you'll have to pass up this step and pay more attention to other indicators during the walkabout. There are so many indicators that you'll still do okay.

Oh mirror, mirror on the wall, what's the fairest roof of all?

You've got to be young or crazy to do this. (This person's one of the above.)

I look closely to see that the roof is designed to keep water from leaking into the interior, that the materials are long-lasting, and that the workmanship is more than adequate — it has to be "good" at least. (I prefer "excellent.")

The advent of rubber sheeting was a blessing for entry-level RVs.

This segmented metal roof was popular in the 70's and early 80's and actually worked quite well. Although on some applications the seams need to be sealed. If the roof is slightly domed for runoff, sealing should not be necessary.

The thin one-piece aluminum roof was problematic because it seeped or leaked wherever a hole was cut for an accessory or vent. Stress at the edges was caused by expansion and contraction from changes in temperature. Being covered with snow was a disaster. Because the metal was only .018 to .022 inches thick and loose fitting, the entire roof often rattled — especially on RVs longer than 25 feet. I was glad to see it virtually disappear.

The rubber roof is forgiving to design and workmanship. If it is well domed and well glued to the underlayment, it should be trouble free and long lasting.

**Fiberglass roof caps have plenty of pluses
and a few minuses.**

Because this molded-fiberglass roof is well
domed, it should give few problems,
provided all attachments are well sealed.

If the roof has a fiberglass insert, which usually means that it is also flat, there are bound to
be problems. It is only slightly domed, if at all. Because RV bodies twist and bend, edge
fastenings tend to loosen. Many sealants don't hold well on fiberglass, so any water pooling
will probably create a leaking problem. In wet climates, I can usually find signs of water
leakage at the ceiling and walls whenever I inspect an RV five years or older that has a
fiberglass insert for a roof covering.

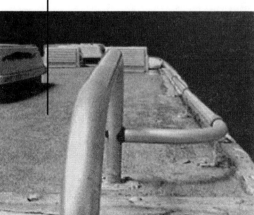

Signs of water pooling are a no-no.

These roofs have water pooling that caused leaks in the interior.

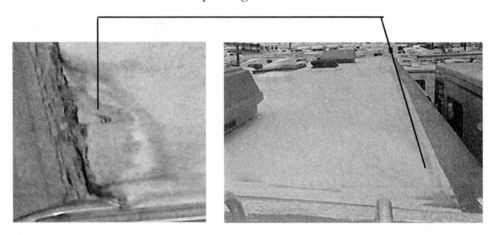

This roof has a good cap and rubber sheeting in the center of the roof. There is a radius trim along the sides to give the effect of a fiberglass cap. However, the trim used to connect the rubber sheeting to the sides acts as a barrier for runoffs and is not adequately sealed. Because water will pool along and inside the trim, this roof will be problematic down the road.

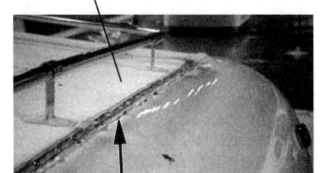

The "out of sight, out of mind" principle allows RV manufacturers to skimp on roofs.

This roof has a serious wrinkle across the center. It might not give a problem, but its presence when new is not a good sign.

This roof has a reasonable runoff, but the rubber sheeting does not extend down the sides. (Notice the sealant along the edge.) If the roof is resealed every 3 or 4 years, there shouldn't be a problem.

This used RV has lots of sealant applied. When you see something like this, be sure to check around the ceiling for signs of water leaks.

If there's no quality on the top, you're bound to have problems sooner or later.

If the roof covering is aluminum, you want it to allow for water runoff. You want the metal to be thick enough so it won't buckle, and it must be well sealed.

Although rubber roofs are easy to seal, they must be well domed to provide for water runoff. Although wrinkles are difficult to avoid in the installation process (and small wrinkles rarely cause problems), serious wrinkles are not good.

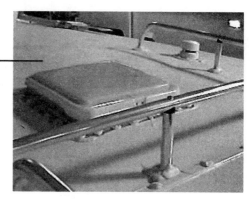

Molded-fiberglass roofs must be well domed because it is quite difficult to seal through-roof accessories. There must be no low spots that allow for water pooling.

Step 5 — Chassis

The chassis involves more than just steel railings and cross pieces. It involves everything that comprises the foundation of the RV from the tires to mechanisms that drive adjuncts like slideout rooms. A good way of thinking about chassis when you're doing a walkabout is that if it's not part of the house, it must be part of the chassis.

Because the chassis is the foundation of the RV, it is crucial to your safety. In motor homes the chassis is definitely safety related. Most current problems with motor homes have to do with being overloaded or uncontrollable (as discussed in chapter 4). In travel trailers — both trailer coaches and fifth wheels — we have many design problems that involve breakage of the chassis at some point. The walkabout won't always tell you about future failures and bad handling characteristics; but because you aren't going to do a walkabout on a brand that has low ratings, you are really looking for indicators that can help you make a *final* decision. Although an understanding of the chassis and its components is technically involved, there are some things that commonly reveal the vehicle's handling characteristics at highway speeds (for both trailers and motor homes), how it will perform in a low-speed collision scenario (motor homes), or how steady it will be when towing (trailers).

Once you've done step 5 by itself a few times, you should do this part of the walkabout combined with step 3 (structure). Once you have gained experience, you can do the left side of the RV — both structure and chassis — before you get to the roof. When you do the right side skin, structure, and chassis, you won't have to go back to the left side. Completing a side at a time is very practical because you have to tie things together anyway, which would include some of step 10 (fixtures). Because chassis is the last step on the outside, you'll soon learn to be a keen observer of things on the inside.

So, use the chassis step as a chance to check on everything that your eyes can see and your fingers can touch. If you just let it flow to your notepad and your brain, you will come away with the impression that will help you in making the right decision.

When under a travel trailer, a quick look at the axles can tell you a lot.

The number of wheels on the ground will give you an idea of the capacity when coupled with tire size. But what you're looking for is the quality of workmanship that was used to attach the axles to the chassis rails. You also might want to look for shock absorbers. No travel trailer should be without them.

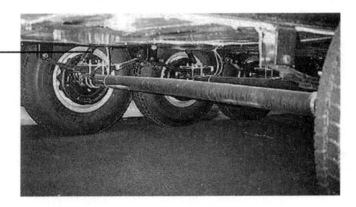

If the attention-to-detail is slack underneath, it's going to be slack all over.

Many times you'll see things that would be okay in a fixed house, but that will never work on an RV bouncing down the road.

Look at the spacing between the tires and think about getting a flat or losing the tread on one tire. I recommend a gap of at least four inches.

Although motor home chassis are complicated, it's important to look them over.

If you don't look, you won't find anything wrong. I had one buyer who told me that she looked under the motor home for the first time five months after she bought it. She couldn't believe the amount of rust she saw. She sent the pictures. They were unbelievable. It looked like the entire chassis had been submerged in salt water. By looking underneath, you will see if something is drastically wrong. After looking a few times, you'll know if wires are sloppily placed or straps are loose. Of these three pictures, notice that in one of them the chassis looks corroded. It's easy to spot.

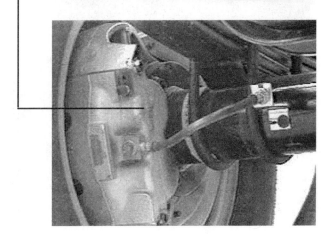

Slideout mechanisms are part of the chassis.

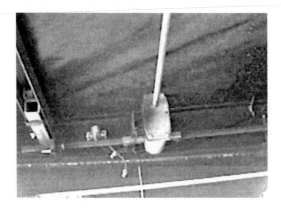

It's important to study the designs, but be sure you look for flaws in the workmanship. You can't always tell if the design is adequate, but you can tell if the assembly process is sloppy. Whatever the builders do, they should do it right.

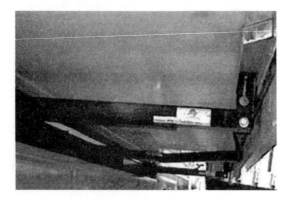

Slideout supports will fail if the parts fail.

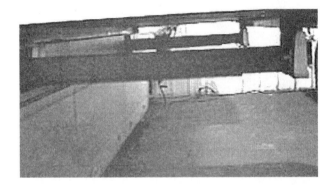

You need to look at more than just the support beams. Bearings and rollers are critical to keeping the slideout from jamming and overloading the drive motor. If the gearing and controls are exposed to dirt, water, and road debris, you will probably have a failure down the road.

While you're under a motor home, take a peek at the low-speed collision bar.

These supports are for the front cap on a class A. They are inadequate for minimizing damage to the front cap or the cockpit area at any speed. You will find some motor homes with heavy metal beams snug to the front cap — which should be effective at impact speeds to 20 miles-per-hour.

Step 6 — Galley

Never discount the galley — which, of course, is the kitchen in a fixed house — it's the heart of live-in activity. The features of the galley go beyond comfort and safety — they encompass your personal health. If the features of the galley are inadequate for the type of use you are anticipating, you are jeopardizing your health, comfort, safety, and overall happiness with the lifestyle. You can see from this list that I take the galley seriously. If the galley isn't right, the RV isn't right. The following pictures and narratives should give you a good idea of how a galley should impact your buying decision.

When Roy Easton and I started doing the walkabout in 1987, we found ourselves putting more emphasis on the galley than we thought we would. Because we were checking out older RVs to get a good picture of the longevity of the various brands — and because at times bad weather forced us to spend more time inside than outside — we gradually moved toward using the galley as an indicator of the general health of the RV. This not only seemed to work, but it became more fun.

Our system has proven itself. Without a good galley the RV won't work for its intended purpose. If the galley design is bad, serious RVers will trade it before they pay it off. If the materials are bad, it won't hold together under varying weather (inside and out) and reasonable use. If the workmanship is bad, it'll start showing defects— much to the owner's frustration. Because we looked at thousands of RVs that were 5 to 10 years old, we were soon convinced that the condition of the galley would tell us much about the rest of the RV.

So, dear reader, don't ignore the galley just because it has a microwave that looks good. Look deep. Spend at least 10 minutes contemplating the scope of your activity when you prepare food and clean up after. If you slack off in the galley, you'll regret it down the road.

When you look at a galley, think of how you'll use it.

Many galleys are designed with as much glitter as efficiency. Don't let this get to you. Ignore the glitz and start your point-by-point inspection.

Galleys must match the rest of the interior design.

It's a matter of taste and practicality. It's like a pair of shoes: If it doesn't fit the rest of the outfit, there's always a feeling that something is wrong.

You'll spend lots of time in the galley, so look closely.

Focus on your use. Will it work for the type of meals you plan to put out?

Look for a good countertop and a good spill-guard all the way around.

Don't get mesmerized by the beauty of it.

Everything added to an RV will add to its cost and its weight. Make sure you aren't buying more than you need.

Keep those spills from wrecking sofas.

Everything looks great here. It has a solid countertop, but notice there's no endcap to prevent spilled liquids from dripping onto the sofa.

This is an entry-level galley but, at least, there's an endcap.

What a nice usable counter with expensive Corian®. If only the manufacturer had spent another $10 for an endcap.

A countertop must be sealed where it contacts the wall.

These two countertops are sealed with a plastic trim (called reverse cove) especially designed for sealing counters to walls. These seals are adequate for entry-level RVs.

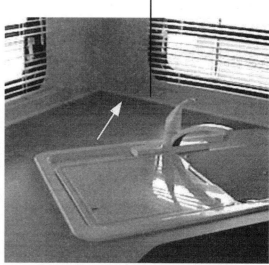

This counter setup is durable and very forgiving to lots of use and abuse. Notice the splashguard next to the walls, the covers for the sink, and a stovetop cover to make the counter larger for food preparation.

Some counter seals do not hold water.

If the RV is used, watch out for warping counters when the seal between the counter and the wall is round bead (gimp). I do not recommend gimp for sealing counters because I know it will leak and it is impossible to clean properly.

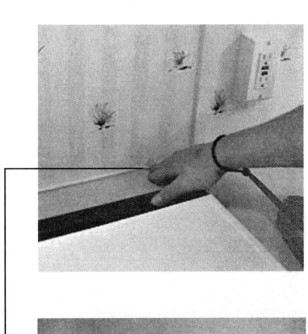

If the seal is flattish with one tight edge on the wall and another tight edge on the counter, it is a reverse cove. Reverse cove is acceptable for vacation class RVs, but I do not recommend it for fulltiming. If it is applied correctly with both edges tight against the surfaces, it will probably be trouble free with reasonable use.

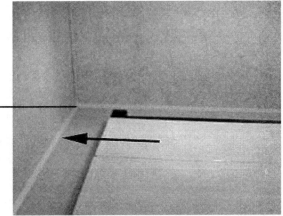

If anything is wrong, it's okay to find it.

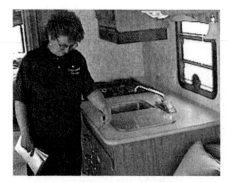

The metal trim around this counter is already loose. Water will get into the composition wood top and cause it to swell.

This very astute appraiser found a big gap under the sink.

TEST: Can you find what's wrong with this counter?

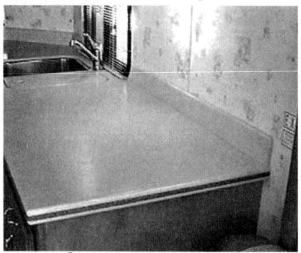

Answer: There's no endcap.

Don't just look at a sink, look into it and touch it.

Like much else in the RV, some things will look good for only a short time. It's not always easy to see, but you need to look. Is stainless as good as plastic? I've found that it depends on the quality of the material. Some plastic sinks are great, some are trash. The same goes for stainless.

Some sinks that look like stainless are actually brushed nickel, and some are made of plastic with a surface that looks like stainless steel.

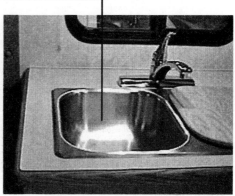

A galley doesn't have to be big and fancy to do its job.

These compact galleys can easily do everything except maybe a Thanksgiving dinner for 10. But don't kid yourself — they are not fulltiming galleys.

Venting is good for spirit and lungs.

A full power vent lke this one will provide good venting for the galley. It is the only venting acceptable for fulltiming use.

Don't confuse air conditioning ducts with exhaust venting.

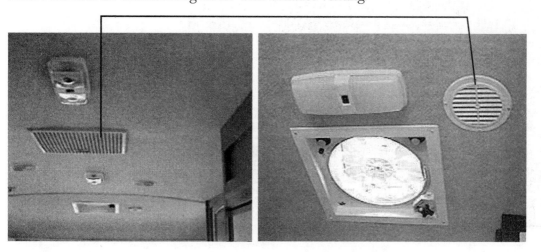

Oh where, oh where do I put my big pots?

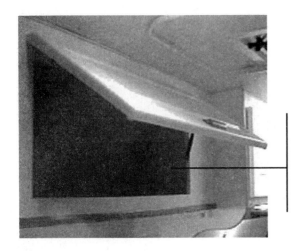

This cabinet over the galley is far from efficient if you can't reach it easily. It might work for paper towels and things you use periodically.

One of these places is good for pots and pans, but the other isn't good for much. Take a few seconds longer to look at storage features.

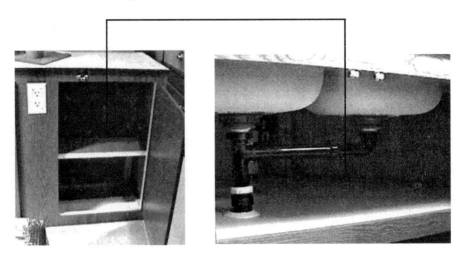

**While in the galley, check out the drawers.
(We'll get to overall woodwork later.)**

This is the type of drawer most often found in fixed homes. It's natural wood and has side-glides.

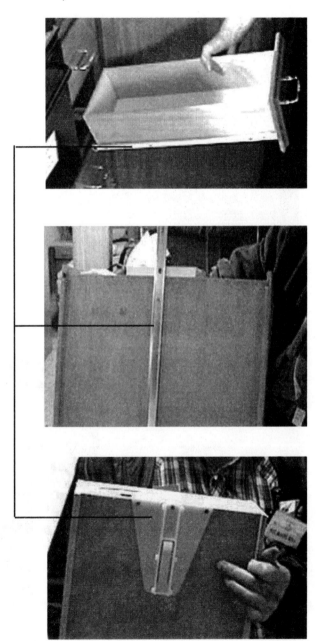

This center guide is metal and it seems to work well, but I don't think it's as smooth or long lasting as one with well-installed side-glides.

This bottom glide is often used on entry-level RVs. It works fine for light service, but it has proven not to last or be durable for heavy-duty service over the long haul.

All drawer glides will have to be well fastened to hold together for twenty years.

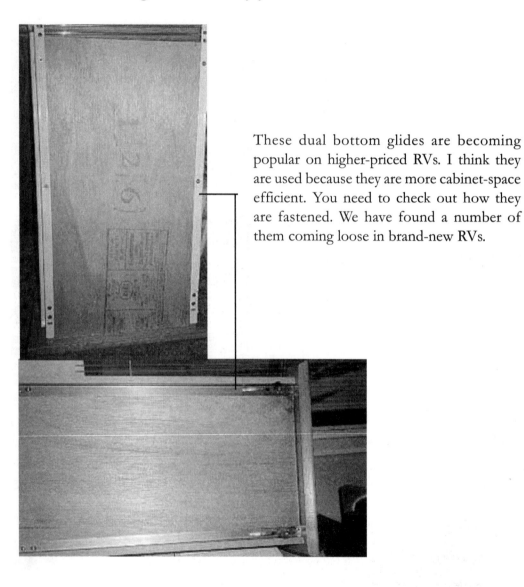

These dual bottom glides are becoming popular on higher-priced RVs. I think they are used because they are more cabinet-space efficient. You need to check out how they are fastened. We have found a number of them coming loose in brand-new RVs.

Moist air makes some drawers swell and smell.

All these drawers have one thing in common, they have composition wood in their makeup. Not only is composition wood heavy, it is not long lasting because it doesn't hold fasteners well. If used in damp climates, composition wood will absorb moisture like a sponge.

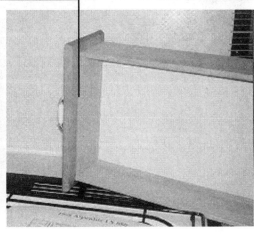

New or used, check those drawers.

I check the drawers to see if they hold together. You should check them for the same reason, plus you'll want to know if they'll work for you. For example, how will you clean this utensils drawer? Maybe you'd be better off with a plastic tray from K-Mart.

Both the drawers below were serviceable, but we found some defects. Check the fasteners to see if they hold the sides to the backplate and faceplate. I find that many of them are loose.

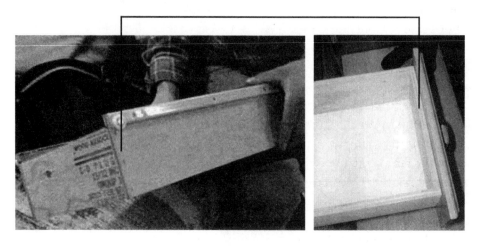

Step 7 — Bathroom

Let's face it, the bathroom is much more than a place to take a bath. Bathrooms are mandatory for modern living. (As opposed to my childhood era.) For most of us it is a place to relax and reflect as we cleanse ourselves inside and out. Therefore, like the galley, the bathroom is important to our comfort and health. The toilet, sink, and shower stall must fit us physically and psychologically. You'd be surprised how our "bringing-up" years influence what we feel about the bathroom. To some, the toilet and bathing area must be totally private. Others are less concerned about privacy and more concerned with function. For these reasons the designers of RVs use various devices, some elaborate, to make bathrooms fit into the psyche of the average RV buyer. In some cases, they design more for looks than for function and durability. RV builders are conscious of the desires of potential buyers when they design floor plans.

As you inspect the bathroom you will want to size it up for you and your family members. You will need to be especially cognizant of the size and layout of the shower stall. As I'll be mentioning throughout this chapter, you will want to look at the way the shower handles water – both incoming and splashing. I am particular, for example, about the height of the shower lining. If it is too low, water will constantly be bombarding the vinyl wall covering above the lining. Of course, I like full-molded shower stalls, but these are generally available only in the more expensive RVs marketed to snowbirds and fulltimers.

In my experience with watching people make decisions on the various models, most take only a cursory look into the bathroom. They spend most of the time with closets, sleeping area, and living room. This is a mistake. How do I know? I know it because I also listen to people when they want to trade their RV in for another one before it's paid off in full. I ask a few questions and invariably the bathroom enters the scene. Some people learn the hard way – you need not be one of them when it comes to bathrooms.

Leaving the shower behind is too traumatic — so we take it with us.

Just because a shower looks good doesn't mean it'll hold up to the rigors of bouncing down the road. Many shower frames are chintzy. You need to inspect them carefully. I grab hold and see if I can rattle the joints.

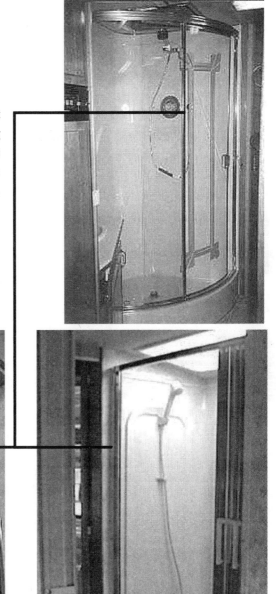

There are showers that look good, and showers that work well.

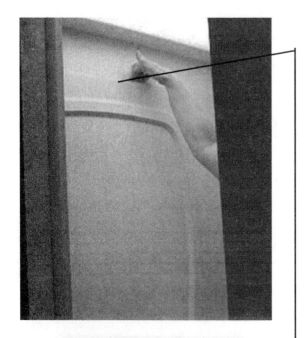

As you can see here, the loose shower lining might allow water to get between it and the wall.

Vinyl will work for vacation use if care is taken not to scrub too much. The thickness of the vinyl is important here.

This should never have happened with only a few years of use.

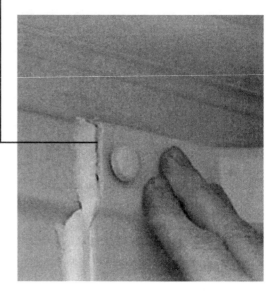

There are shower stalls that work only for limited use.

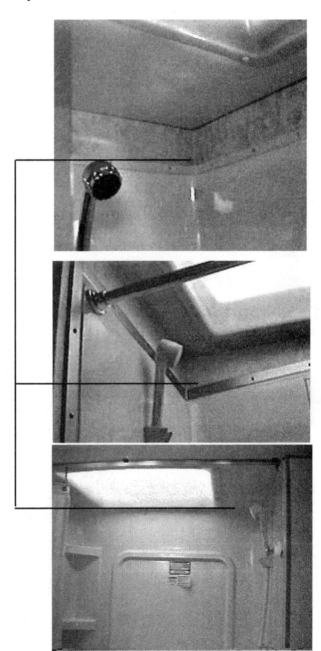

You need to consider your size when you inspect the shower. If you are tall and like good showers, be sure the top of the stall will not catch water and allow it to get behind the fiberglass.

A well-designed shower tub will not let water spill onto the floor.

Shower curtains only work well with deep tubs. With shallow tubs you'll need a shower enclosure that keeps water in the tub and not on the floor. Constantly getting water on the floor will lead to serious problems down the road.

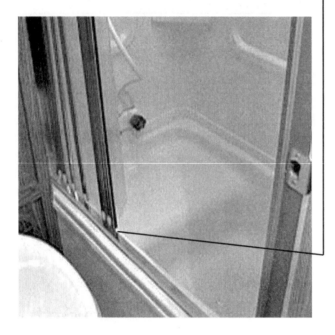

Shower tubs need to be tough, with water-tight enclosures.

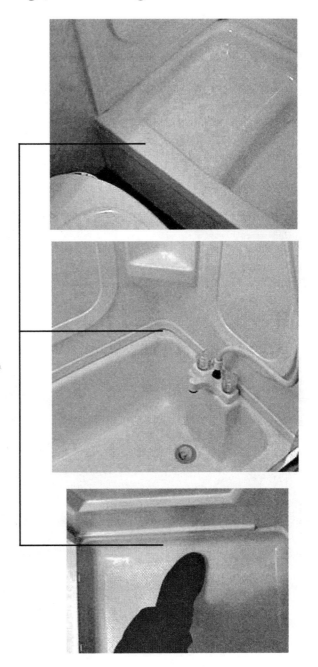

Because there's no enclosure, this won't work.

This wraparound shower stall works extremely well for most applications. Some fulltimers, however, prefer the molded stall because it's easier to clean — and it's more "homelike." The open area between the tub and the shower wall will not leak because the tub has a lip to prevent water from getting into the wall.

I always stomp on tub floors to be sure they aren't soft. Soft floors will eventually fatigue and crack.

Good venting is good for body and spirit.

When you start looking, you're going to be surprised how often you'll find no power vent in the bathroom or even in the vicinity of the bathroom. This is bad for health and comfort.

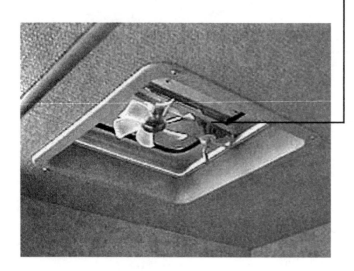

At a very minimum, you need a small power vent in the bathroom. This is the standard fan used for roof venting in entry-level RVs.

Good vents take it all out, and some vents even bring the good stuff back in.

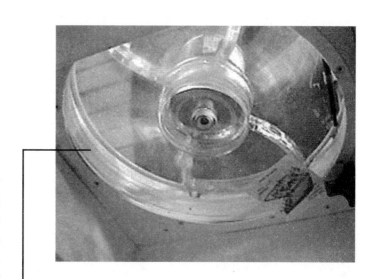

Full-vent fans are the only power fans recommended for serious RVing — and are a must for fulltiming. There are various types of controls. Some are for exhaust only and some both exhaust and intake air. Some have temperature-sensitive and moisture-sensitive controls. They are absolutely fantastic!

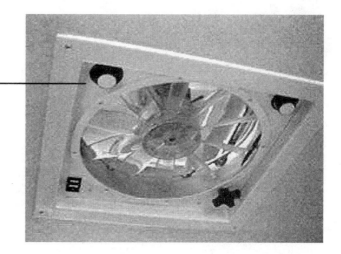

Let there be light!

Skylights are great in RVs when they are right. If they lose too much heat or get too hot, they are inefficient. If they leak, they definitely aren't good. If they are designed so that condensation gets into the wall, you might be looking at serious problems down the road.

Bathroom sinks need to work.

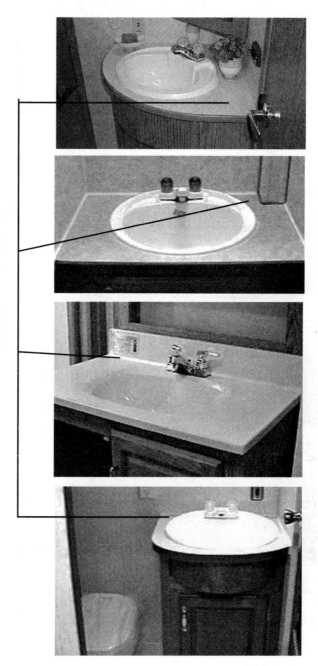

Although bathroom sinks are designed for one person at a time, they need to be workable for washing up or brushing teeth. They also should be easy to clean. Bathrooms that can't be cleaned lead to unhealthy occupants. Can you see which one of these four cannot be properly cleaned?

Call it what you will: head, toilet, or commode.

I've always said that comfort begins with design. This design works for some, but will it work for you?

The big question is:
WILL YOU FIT?

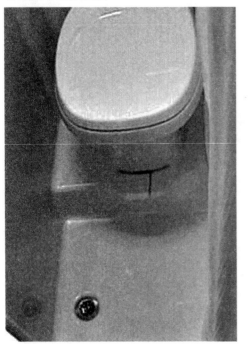

Carpet looks nice, but can be a problem for those with bad aim.

Step 8 — Woodwork

This is the step most buyers cut back on. It's almost as if they're afraid of looking and finding defects. Many tell me that they don't expect RVs to be perfect, so they forgive and forget — until things go wrong after the purchase.

Woodwork covers everything made of wood in the interior. It includes cabinets, drawers, wardrobes, partitions, shelving, and even furniture. When you begin your inspection of woodwork, you must focus on just that. If you get distracted by other things, you won't do a good job. Even though you've looked at some woodwork when you inspected the galley and bath, this step is a new approach. You are going to spend at least 10 minutes with fingers, flashlight, and mirror to check every nook and cranny.

Because of my experience, I probably find many deficiencies that you won't. I do a lot of touching to find out if something is loose that shouldn't be loose. I feel where I can't see to find out if there any hidden defects. In a used RV I sniff around to find out if there's mildew from leaking water. When I do these things every time I go through an inspection, I always find something wrong – even though not all are serious defects.

There is a part of woodwork that is not covered within this chapter because it is a new "science" for the RVCG staff. We have only recently been able to prove that the quality of the woodwork in the interior is critical to the structural integrity of the RV. This is extremely important to class A motor homes. We are finding that, during a rollover scenario, the interior supports the walls. In essence, the interior cabinets and partitions act as gussets to prevent the sidewalls from collapsing. So, don't ignore the strength of the wood and the workmanship that holds it in place. It has as much to do with safety as with beauty.

Before you begin with the fingers, use a wide angle.

Give the decor a once-over with emphasis on woodwork. When you stand back and take a broad look, you might see that things aren't in sync. Wood colors and grains often don't match. Too much glass, too much white, or too much clutter may not fit in an RVing atmosphere.

Let your fingers tell the story.

Get your fingers involved in the inspection process. Use a mirror to see how the framing is fastened. Use your fingers to feel the fasteners or thickness of the vinyl wrap.

There's a place where gimp works and a place where it doesn't.

Gimp (round bead) works well between cabinets and walls to cover slight imperfections, but it does not work well at all around countertops. Gimp is not a water seal.

Good joints: Good chance of good life.

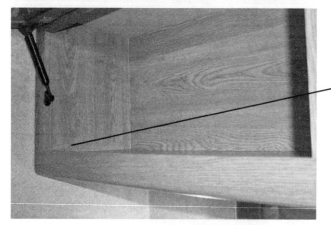

These are good joints that should last for at least 20 years of reasonable use. Whether the joints are tongue-and-groove or simply stapled, much has to do with the workmanship and the materials used. I have seen the best materials fail because the workmanship on the joints was terrible. I have also seen many cabinets with well-stapled picture-frame joints last for 30 years of hard use.

When bad joints get old, they come apart.

Although it is not as common as it used to be, we still see lots of bad joints. Some show splitting because the wood hasn't been properly cured, while others are loose because the workmanship was bad.

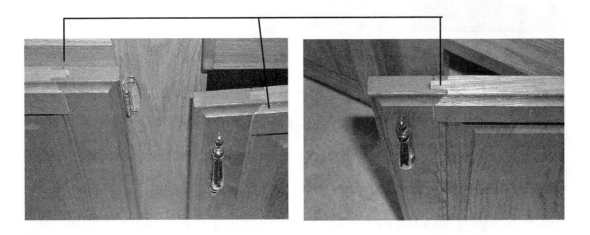

To last or not to last? That is the question.

We find loose trim and we find doors that hit things when they open. If you find it's wrong, you can decide whether you want to live with it. If you don't find it now, you will later.

Keep checking those drawers.

Sometimes the wood looks like it's natural but, upon closer examination, it's composition wood.

Just because the RV has side slides on drawers in the galley, it doesn't mean it'll be that way in the bedroom.

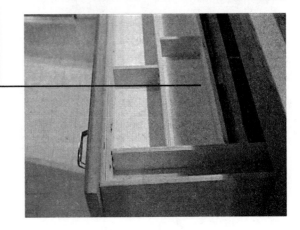

These divided drawers look practical, but they rarely work well in real life.

If it's not good, it will go bad.

When you buy an RV, you may expect a few things to go wrong, but you aren't happy when they do. If you keep the RV from 5 to 10 years, you will be very unhappy if things like those shown here multiply each year. When you see things like this in an RV under 5 years old, you should question the quality of the brand.

Step 9 — Lining

Once you step through the door of an RV, you are within a container. Remember I told you how Roy and I coined some words to make the steps simple for our simple brains? (Well, at least mine.) To us, the floor, the ceiling, and the interior walls compose the inside lining of a container — which in this case is the RV. Now that you've gone to the galley, inspected the bathroom, and checked out the woodwork, you probably have a pretty good idea whether this RV is for you. In case the RV is still on your worth-considering list, it's time to take a fresh look at the inside. It's time to look closely at the interior walls. It's time to look upward and see if there are defects in the ceiling. It's time to concentrate on the floor covering. If you buy this RV, you'll find out within six months whether you've made the right choice. After you own it, it's too late to start wishing.

In most new RVs, you'll see indicators of the lack of attention-to-detail, while in used RVs you'll see many deficiencies. If you really want to get a good idea of how the RV will look five years down the road, look at a dozen or so used ones of the same brand. Make the lining step a priority. Just walk in and walk through while allowing your eyes to catch the inside surfaces and corners. Look into the cabinets for water stains. Look under the sink for indications of plumbing leaks. Look around the wardrobes and partitions for loose paneling. You'll find more wrong than you can imagine, and it'll start you thinking.

It's important that you begin this step the same way each time. I usually go back to the entrance area and just stand there for a minute or two. As I turn and reflect on my inspection up to this point, I am comparing the brand with other brands. I am formulating a number in my head, but I don't make it solid until I walk through once again to check the walls, ceiling, and floor for things that are wrong. Notice that I am saying "wrong." This is a good time to change your focus from looking for positives to looking for negatives. You need to do this at some point or the entire check won't be objective. Ask yourself, "What could be wrong with this RV?" It should take you no more than five minutes to do this step, but it could be a very valuable five minutes.

There are defects — even if you don't see them.

No RV is perfect. The most "perfect" RV doesn't show its defects because they are not obvious. What you are looking for is any defect that is a symptom of bad design, materials, or workmanship.

Your eyes like straight lines.

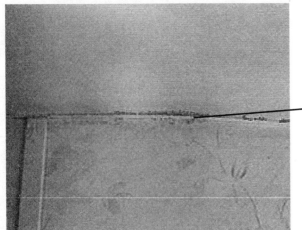

You may not see it from a distance, but when you look close, it'll be there.

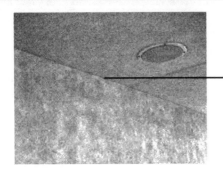

When the ceiling line isn't straight, it will never look right.

You won't find flaws at the ceiling line if you don't look. Believe me, if you find it after the purchase, you will see it constantly. Sometimes the cause is just a workmanship defect while other times it's a more serious design deficiency.

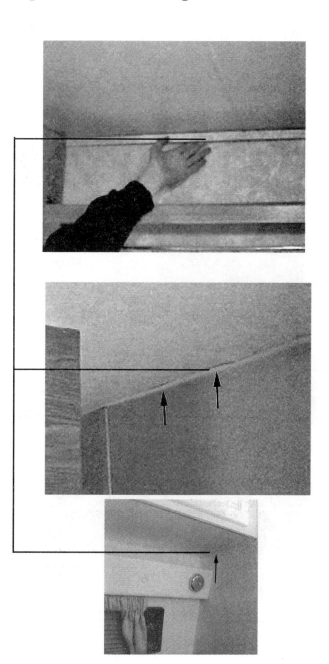

Some stains are easy to find.

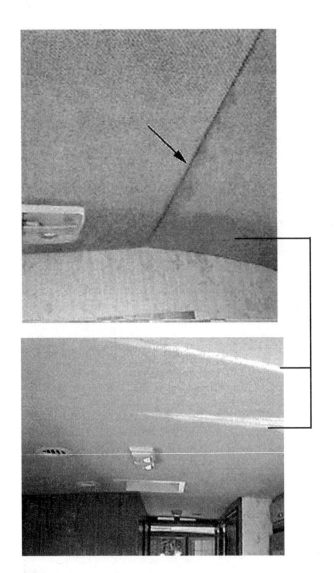

Some stains and wrinkles draw your eye like a magnet. These stains are serious. If you are still interested in the RV, you need to be sure the leak has been fixed, that there is no permanent damage, and that the stains can be removed. Wrinkles are difficult to fix.

Some stains are hard to find.

Some water leaks are seepers. They leak every time it rains but not enough to form puddles on the floor. Eventually, signs emerge through wrinkles in the ceiling or stains on the fabric. Often these stains are inside the cabinets next to the wall. You need to be a bit of a detective to find the smaller ones.

Serious stains are signs of serious problems.

Sometimes you can clean the stains from the ceiling, but the wood still shows that it doesn't like being water soaked.

Not only does moisture rot wood, it also grows fungus.

When an RV is constantly wet inside, all wood will begin to absorb some of the moisture. Once it gets into the wood, it is practically impossible to eliminate. There is, however, one way to kill the fungus: Leave it in the Southwestern Desert for an entire summer — preferably in Death Valley.

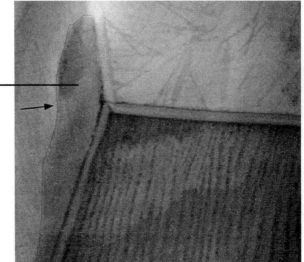

The floor must be strong — the covering tough.

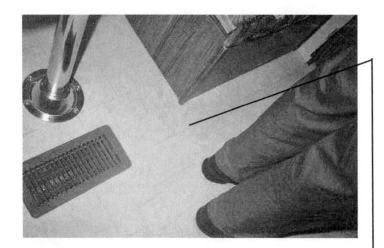

As you inspect the floor covering, stomp on it to be sure that it has a solid foundation.

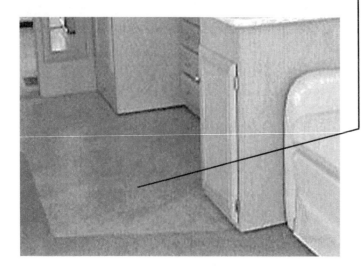

The floor covering in the galley must be both washable and durable.

Many floor coverings are for show.

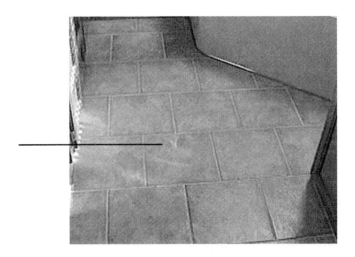

The bouncing and concentrated activity is hard on any floor, but it has been proven that tile, wood, and parquet floor coverings generally don't work for long in an RV. All these floors are under 10 years old and are showing extensive wear and other problems.

What's underfoot should never be taken for granted.

Feel the firmness of the floor as you study the walls and the ceiling. Cast your eyes downward occasionally to see if the design, workmanship, and materials are what you can live with. Like a good tool, a floor covering should take hard use with a minimum amount of maintenance.

Step 10 — Fixtures

Everything in the RV that is fastened to the floor, wall, and ceiling is considered a fixture. And you should know by now that everything built into an RV must somehow be fastened to the floor, wall, or ceiling. Anything loose will eventually be damaged. In motor homes anything not solidly fastened to the floor, wall, or ceiling is a definite safety hazard. Fixtures include appliances, utilities (furnace, water heater, air conditioner, converters, inverters, generators, plumbing, wiring, etc.), lighting fixtures, and furniture. Because the list is long, you can see that this step is actually an overview of the entire interior and possibly some features of the exterior. By the time you get to this step, you should be ready to give the RV one good, long final look to decide whether a model is worth putting on your to-be-considered list. From the pictures you'll be looking at now, you should get the impression that the fixtures step (remember, it's an overview) will determine whether you're going to give the model you've been inspecting a thumbs-up or a thumbs-down.

Because I rate every RV I inspect with a 1 to 10 score, I must be sure that I am fair in my evaluation. This is the way I try to be fair: I have made it a habit not to judge any model by the brand rating that I know exists. I must have justification for any number that pops into my head or appears on my scorecard. If I can't find anything wrong during my complete walkabout, I know it will get a 10. If it has a few things wrong and it's five years old, then it would probably get an 8 or 9 — depending on the problems and the age of the RV. It might not be as scientific as RVCG's method, but it does give me a basis for forming an impression of a brand — which is part of my job.

You also can rate the RV. But you should rate it according to what you think it will do for you. Where I ignore color, you must consider the color. Where I ignore floor plan, you must consider floor plan. Where I ignore size of bathroom and bedroom, these are things you must consider. You must also leave with an impression, but it should be of both the brand and model.

So stop and take a deep breath. This is an opportunity for serious concentration. This is where you need to focus at wide angle. You take it all in before you begin the final countdown.

Look around before you make the final plunge.

By now you know that all slideout rooms add weight to the RV, and overhead TVs compromise the safety of motor home occupants. These are two items that will influence your choice.

You know many things by now, because you've gone this far. But because you're not at the end, you need to walk through once again to check a few items that you might have missed, and a few new ones. They are all there just waiting for you.

Your eyes will probably hit the furniture first.

Some fabrics don't work in an RV because of concentrated use. Because re-upholstering is expensive, choose the fabric carefully.

Check out the location of the furniture in relation to the galley. A stained sofa will dramatically depreciate the value of the RV.

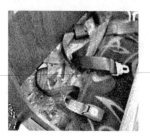

In motor homes, always check the seat belts. Those attached to the sofas are installed at the discretion of the RV manufacturer. I like to see how the seatbelts are mounted into the floor.

In a trailer or motor home, furniture needs to be fastened to floor or wall.

It's easy to check the furniture to see if it's fastened.

Some furniture are solidly fastened with steel bolts into the floor while some use simple straps or bungee cords tied to the wall.

Location of chairs, as you see here, can give you a big headache.

By jove, we can't forget the stove.

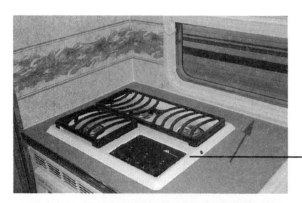

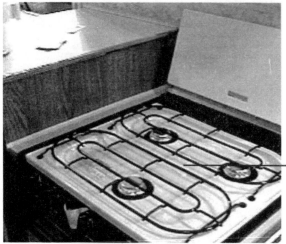

Stoves used to vary in price and quality. Unfortunately, RV stoves are pretty much locked up by one manufacturer. Their representative told me that they stopped building good stoves when they found out RVers didn't care about stove quality. When I disputed this, he just walked off. All RV stoves are now made for light use. Check it out carefully, then consider it a "camping" stove.

This one's great for a weekend when heating beans is the chore of the day.

The appliances should be of household quality.

Not everyone who goes RVing needs a big refrigerator, washer/dryer, and microwave — but some do. If you don't need these, you will have needlessly impacted space, weight, and money. But if you need them, check them out just as you would when looking at appliances for a fixed home. Quality should not be compromised. Look at the brand name on the appliances. Failures of these products are major sources of frustration for serious RVers.

Look at those miscellaneous things that make life easier.

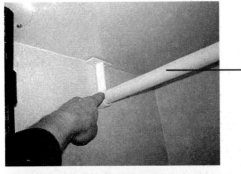

I find many hanging bars for holding clothes and towels that are not properly fastened to the wall. Some simply are screwed into thin paneling. Good manufacturers have plates in the wall that support these fixtures.

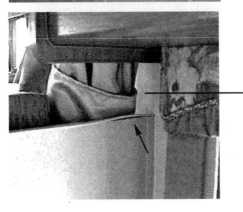

Be sure to look closely at the quality of things added to "dress" the RV for appearance.

To ignore lighting is to stumble.

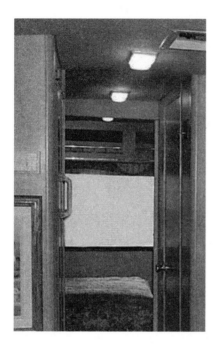 

Be sure all lighting is practical and not just there to sell the RV. I have heard of manufacturers adding lighting simply to please the dealers who wanted the RV to "show" better. The quality of the fixtures is often not as good as that found in a fixed dwelling.

Many pass up things that may appear boring, but don't you do it.

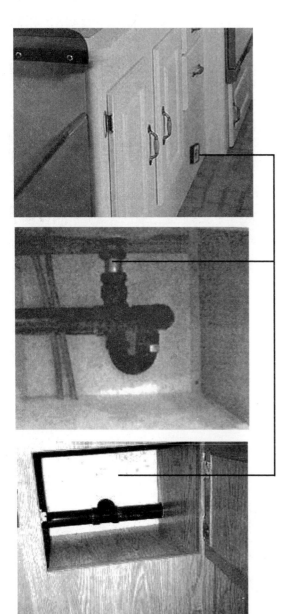

In this picture there is a small panel that "sniffs" the levels of propane and/or carbon monoxide in the air. You need to know it is there because it should be there.

Plumbing joints should be accessible. It never hurts to check them out . You might be surprised at what you find — right or wrong.

Don't ignore things that could be a pain-in-the . . . later.

Few furnaces are exposed like this one, but you should at least locate it. I found one that had the firebox too close to the wood paneling. It had already started charring the wood.

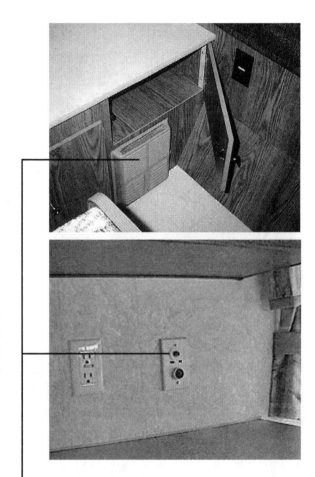

Wiring, electrical outlets, and gas piping are difficult to check out completely, but if you open a cabinet and see these things, take a few seconds to look them over.

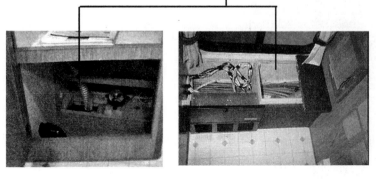

Overhead TVs are DEADLY!

Cockpits should be designed with safety in mind. RV manufacturers, unfortunately don't think this way. It's left up to you to set them right. If you think the risk to your safety is too high with an overhead TV, you have other choices.

There is a safe place for a TV in the cockpit.

If you ignore the TV location before you buy, you might think about it later and feel uncomfortable every time you drive the RV.

These are good locations. Newer RVs will often have the TV in an entertainment center — a good location away from the cockpit.

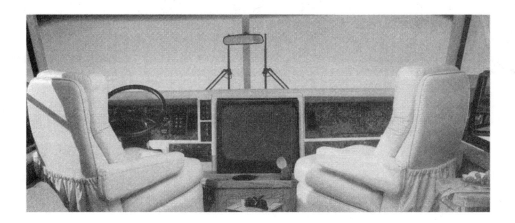

Conclusion:

The walkabout is designed to keep you from buying an RV with which you'll be dissatisfied. However, there's no way that you're going to spot everything wrong with the RV. Some things you won't know and some things you won't see. But that's okay. You'll see the things that are most important to your final decision about whether you want to take a chance on a brand or a particular unit. And that's your goal. If you live by the ratings, you'll know what satisfaction polls, used appraisals, and new evaluations are saying. Your job is not to look at thousands or even hundreds of RVs. Your job is to carefully inspect the RV you are considering. Your job will be to choose an RV that you will feel good about for the next five to ten years.

The walkabout will be the last step of the pre-buying stage, but it won't end there. You will also find yourself automatically doing a walkabout on the particular vehicle for which you are negotiating. You'll find yourself doing a complete walkabout after you've signed the papers — but before you take it away from the dealership. Even though your emotions will be high during the buying stage, you'll find that a walkabout is a good way to cool your head and maybe the buying process. Unless you feel truly good about a particular RV, you won't want to buy it.

So, now that you've learned the basics of doing a walkabout, go ahead and do a few. Take this book and have at it. After you feel comfortable with what you've learned, go boldly where all RVers eventually must go — into the buying arena.

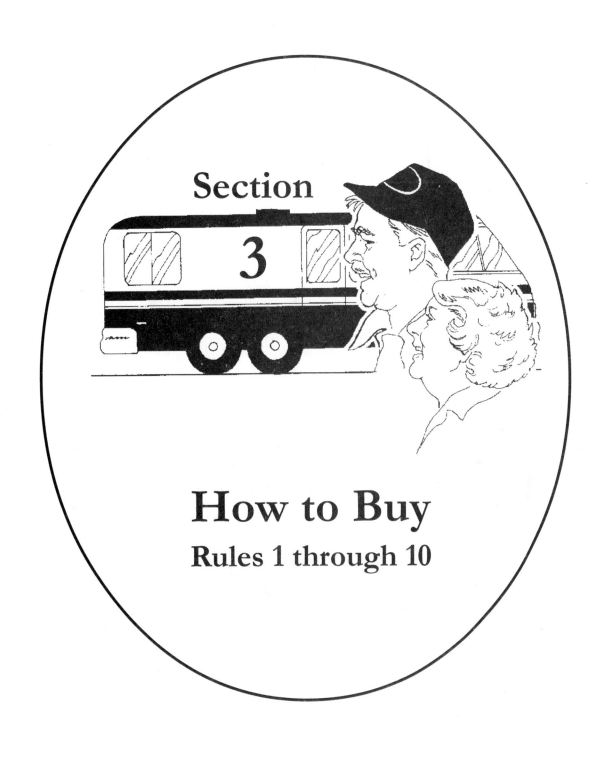

Section 3

How to Buy

Rules 1 through 10

Introduction to How to Buy

Buying an RV requires the same techniques as buying a car, a truck, a boat, a mobile home, or real estate. The salespeople come from the same mold. The business owners have similar philosophies. You and your neighbor have buying habits that could probably be exchanged without notice. Therefore, what you learn in this section alone should save you hundreds of times the cost of this book.

The ten rules outlined in this section are easy to follow. I have students who have made unbelievable buys while getting what they need and want by following these ten rules. This section is meant to be compact; so if you have to slow down now and then think about what's being said, consider it normal. Reference material is noted in the text and in the back of the book.

Following the ten rules will pit you against the odds of throwing away at least $6,000 — the amount the average buyer throws away by buying wrong or paying too much. The rewards for accepting this adventure head-on will be great. You'll go further and be happier. You'll be proud of yourself for buying right. You'll make friends by helping others. The adventure will never stop.

If I write a bit harshly about RV salespeople, please don't judge me too fast. I've been on many sales lots as a consumer and as a salesperson. Every day I hear horror stories of people who have lost most of their savings to the hot-shots. That I have a bias for the RV consumer is not in question. I freely admit it. After you've read the book completely and followed the rules in this section, you can write to me and tell me if you think I'm off base.

The following is part of a commentary on RV discount houses that I wrote for an RV Consumer Group newsletter some years ago. These excerpts might help illustrate my viewpoint about RV salespeople.

saw one get caught in grand style. This young man got caught because the element of urgency was there. His dream was to take his young family on a cross-country trip before the progression of serious illness in one of the family members prevented this dream from happening. It was a now or never scenario. He got caught in the web.

His statement was: *"I would never believe it could happen to me. With my vast experience in handling people, I was smoothly manipulated by an expert. I believed him when he said it was an unbelievable buy. He was trustable. He was smooth. I bit. I don't like what I bought, and I paid $15,000 too much. I just don't believe I did it."*

I saw another get caught in the web. This one was snared so quickly and tightly that I'm not sure he ever knew what happened. This "well-experienced" RVer left with a 350 C.I.D. (5.7L) Chevrolet engine pulling an 11,000 Gross Vehicle Weight Rating (GVWR) fifth wheel — and the 3/4 ton truck had a short bed! (Specification per GM is 8,400 pounds maximum trailer weight.) When I saw the trailer leaving on a downhill slope, it couldn't even make a 70-degree turn from the lot without hitting the truck cab. Both truck and trailer were new. One of the two would have to be replaced at a big loss. I heard the statement from the salesperson on this one. *"Put in an RV cam,"* he said, *"and it'll work fine. I'll even deduct the cost from the trailer price."* The buyer wanted to believe. He was still believing when I last saw him.

I was appraising a 2-year-old fifth wheel when an older couple walked in to take another look at their purchase of a few minutes before. *"We weren't ready to buy until fall,"* the small gray-haired lady said, *"but it's so pretty and the price is so good that we decided to buy today."* The couple paid about $15,000 and the book retail was closer to $10,000. When I finished the appraisal on their unit, the score was 3 on a scale of 1 to 10 — with 10 being the highest.

This couple didn't know about the quality of RVs because they had never owned one. They judged the RV from a narrow perspective, and they trusted the salesperson to take care of their needs. That the ceiling had major defects would have been impossible for them to know. They hadn't reviewed *The RV Ratings Guide CD* so they couldn't know this particular manufacturer doesn't do very well at putting RVs together.

Not everyone gets caught. One buyer confided that he caught the salesperson changing direction with each RV entered. *"He was smooth at it,"* he said. *"If I hadn't been on the ball, I would have been taken in. He was so good that I might have bought. I knew just enough to catch him."*

RVers need to know enough to stay out of the web. They need to know if the deal is fair. They need to buy right at a dealership that can service their needs. Part of the sales presentation should be about the dealership — its service, its history, its future — and the salesperson. RVers need to be happy about their purchase for more than six months.

There are those who believe that bursting the bubble will blow the dream. Not so! Bursting the bubble that all RVs are the same will make for happier RVing. Bursting the bubble that all RV salespeople can be trusted will help get RVers into the right RVs. Bursting the bubble that you get a better deal on price alone will help RV consumers make better buying decisions.

Bursting the bubble will help some — but not all. On a sunny day, it's easy to get caught in the web.

About Smoothy

Now, something about Smoothy, the main character in this section. Smoothy is a composite of real salespeople. Smoothy exists. The statements quoted came from the mouths of real Smoothies. Don't expect Smoothy to be a man or a woman. Don't expect Smoothy to be young or old. Don't expect Smoothy to smile, to frown, to be friendly, or unfriendly. Don't expect Smoothy to be talkative, to be smart, or to like you. Smoothy is only one  thing: a practitioner of getting you into an RV at Smoothy's profit.

If you think you know who Smoothy is, you're wrong — unless, of course, you signed the papers then came off the high. You only know Smoothy after the fact. Like a doctor who does nothing for you, but does a lot to you. Like a lawyer who holds out his hand after losing a case that couldn't be lost.

There is only one way to find and outsmart Smoothy: follow the ten rules in this section. Because you want to go RVing, I know you will accept the challenge. You've got to deal before you wheel.

Chapter 15

*Rule 1:
Prepare to
choose in the
correct order!*

T
he correct order for choosing an RV is as follows: **1) type, 2) size, 3) quality, 4) floor plan, and 5) price.** Most RVers make serious mistakes in more than one of these areas. The proof is in the number of almost-new RVs on the sales lots. Every RV traded before five years costs the owner thousands of dollars. Consider:

Buying wrong results in nonuse.
Buying wrong causes changes in travel plans.
Buying wrong results in frustration.
Buying wrong makes for a poor investment.
Buying wrong makes Smoothy richer — and you poorer.

Although the investment in your RV is influenced by all five areas, size is the number one reason for change with type a close second. When it comes to changing, it seems that motor homes win first place. (It may be like Thanksgiving dinner — bigger eyes than stomach.)

When you look at an RV, your emotions will get in the way of your needs. It will happen. The anticipation of going over the next hill or into the wilderness will tend to cloud conservative buying habits. It happens to all of us. To make a good buy, logic must overpower emotion.

How far ahead should I plan?

If you don't have a time frame, it's almost impossible to have good direction. History has proven that RVers generally trade within five years with big losses. Societal changes have a big impact. The statement, *"I plan on keeping it for twenty years,"* is rarely heard today because it sounds silly. Unfortunately, some RV manufacturers are taking advantage of this trend by building disposable RVs. This marketing technique compounds the problem of premature failures and extreme waste at a time when old RVs are plaguing the countryside.

You need to look five years into your personal future. Look at your desire to travel. Look at your enjoyment of primitive camping. Try to determine the kind of campgrounds where you'll be staying. To help determine where you're going, study the maps of North America — always include Canada and Mexico in your 5-year plan. If you plan on going easterly more than westerly, you may want a different size or type. If you plan on snowbirding or fulltiming, you'll definitely need to look seriously at quality, size, and floor plan.

If you ignore the 5-year plan, it'll be like buying a house without checking the foundation. You would never do that — would you?

Plan 5 years ahead!

Why choose type first?

Don't even begin to get serious until you decide on the type of RV you'll need for your RVing adventures. Salespeople will try to influence you, your friends will try to influence you, and your neighbors will tell you what they think. Most will add to the confusion. If you keep in mind that the type of RV you choose is the very first aspect of the buying decision, you'll be more apt to sift information when you and your spouse sit alone. You must consider type, size, quality, floor plan, and price to prepare for your 5-year plan, but always keep type ahead of the rest.

Let's face it, isn't the quality pretty much the same in all brands?

If manufacturers and salespeople could convince you of this, their lives would be easier. That all brands are not created equal can be easily proven on your own by following the simple guidelines you'll be studying in Rule 5. If you don't think you can do well at appraising, use *The RV Ratings Guide CD* as your guide.

Salespeople usually try to avoid questions of comparison. When you ask about brands, Smoothy will hem and haw. Watch his eyes when you get into the subject. From the basic knowledge you begin to accumulate, you'll be able to make a good judgement on whether his words are credible opinion or bull.

No RV is good enough. You might as well begin to believe it now because you're going to find out it's a fact of life.

It's not hard to check an RV on your own. All of my students learn to check two areas that set the pulse for quality: the galley and the roof. If you use *The RV Ratings Guide CD* as a gauge for safety and quality, don't waste your time on RVs rated below 70 — unless it's to satisfy curiosity.

If you find your tastes developing beyond the strength of your checkbook, you may want to stay with the quality standard and switch to a good used RV. Keep in mind that 90% of RVers make big mistakes and want to trade within the 5-year time frame. Many of these RVs are as good as new. It takes a bit more work to find a good one with an acceptable floor plan for you, but the savings are often tremendous. If, however, you are planning on buying almost new, you still should make comparisons with new.

When all else fails,
stay in budget!

What if the only floor plan I like is in a lower quality RV?

Floor plans are never perfect. You'll find the worst manufacturers can have some of the best floor plans — because they ignore basic construction techniques required for efficient use and good handling. You will most assuredly find the cheapest RVs loaded with cabinets and wardrobes. These manufacturers won't tell you there's no way you can use them without throwing the vehicle out of balance or that the payload capacity is nowhere near enough to fill these storage areas with anything except pillows. Compromises will probably have to be made — especially in the areas of storage and capacity. Once you're on the road, you'll learn very fast that you can't take everything you own with you.

Study the floor plans. Be sure the brochures have details you can understand when you review them at home. Until you make up your mind on type, you'll have to compare floor plans of travel trailer coaches, fifth wheels, and motor homes. You'll soon see there are obvious differences that limit floor plans in some types.

If you come across a Smoothy in the first stages of your investigation, you'll find yourself being encouraged to sit in the driver's seat of a motor home. You'll think of yourself as an airplane pilot — having the thrill of pushing but-

I really like this one, but I can't see a place where I can store all my tools.

There's always a compromise!

tons and pulling levers as you control this vehicle while zooming down the highway toward great adventures. If Smoothy knows of a bonus on a trailer with particularly big windows, he'll draw pictures in your mind of the beautiful view you'll have as you sit on the rim of a great canyon or by the side of a wilderness lake. If he thinks he can get you excited over a runabout motor home, you'll find him pushing the practicality of good mileage and easy access to shopping center parking spaces. All of this needs to be pointed out, but the floor plan that seems practical on the sales lot might not work in real RVing.

Many neophytes get locked into a specific bed and bath configuration. Consider that twin beds are usually very efficient but can make spouses into strangers. Consider that front-to-rear walk-around beds are roomier but consume a lot of floor space. Consider that corner beds are space efficient but almost impossible to make up in the morning. Consider that small corner baths get old too soon, but that the larger rear baths eliminate tail-end views. The list is almost endless for compromises. It's something that has to be worked out carefully without pressure from others. The floor plan is the most personal decision of the five areas — and the major reason for premature trading.

Why is price last when everyone else puts it first?

The price is tied to your budget — and there's an RV for every budget. People get caught up in price because it's easy for dealers to advertise price and salespeople to sell on price. Price gets attention everywhere. Ninety percent of RVers look at price as number one. Once you focus on price, everything else takes a back seat. You need to replace price with budget. You need to counter the influences being pushed at you. The price will be forgotten as you see the cabinetry show premature wear. The price will be forgotten as you complain about the floor plan. The price will be forgotten as you realize you should have bought something else.

To accurately figure budget you need to stay focused on your crystal ball. Your budget should include everything for the next five years. It should be accurate within 10%. The list will be long and will take hours of work; but since Smoothy will almost always use price to get you to the closing desk, you'll need to stay focused on your budget. Price is not a major concern until you decide upon type, size, quality and floor plan — in that order.

If you sleep on the budget, Smoothy will get you!

Sure, a motor home will cost a lot if you don't use it. If you drive it, it'll pay for itself in five years. I put 30,000 miles on mine in two years.

Smoothy rarely knows anything about RVing that he hasn't learned on the sales lot. If Smoothy has traveled at all with an RV, all his learning has been haphazard at best.

The average mileage per year for motor homes before heavy depreciation takes place is about 4,000 miles. You'll pay dearly for each mile over that average. How much would you pay for a 4 year-old motor home that has 50,000 on the odometer? It surely wouldn't be anywhere near the value of the same motor home with 16,000 miles. If you bring in a trade that has above average miles, watch Smoothy knock the dollars off the trade-in allowance.

Chapter 16

Rule 2:

Have 5 test questions ready

Prepare five questions to ask each RV salesperson you meet. You must, of course, know the answers — and, please, don't make them too easy. Any salesperson earning between $40,000 and $100,000 annually should be a professional able to answer almost any question you can throw at him or her.

Don't be led and don't believe everything you hear. It's too early in the game to trust the players. You may need to fight the temptation to be nice. Think about the hard work it took to get the money you're planning to spend on this RV. Let's make it your decision all the way.

The questions you ask should pertain to your 5-year plan. If they are important, your sincerity will show to the salesperson. Some people take notes during the presentation — others afterward. You should do it according to your comfort zone. The notetaking is secondary — your feelings about the salesperson as a professional are paramount.

Don't let yourself feel guilty about putting on the pressure. The person standing before you (male or female) earns at least $30 per hour — every hour! Don't expect less from an RV salesperson than you would from an RV technician.

If you don't have questions ready, you will never be in control of the buying process. Being in control means that you will probably be one of those who keeps the $6,000 throwaway going. It all begins here. A few hours of preparation will save you thousands of dollars. Do it!

Should I ask these questions at first or spread them out?

You'll want to spread out your questions, but try to do it within the first 30 minutes. Since you're not yet an expert, don't give the salesperson a hint of where you're going. Your job at this time is solely to eliminate the salesperson who can't help you.

Begin by finding out how long the salesperson has been in the business. If he's a beginner, there's room for forgiveness. If he's been at it for years and still doesn't know anything, you should beware. All salespeople should know RV basics. Always ask if he owns an RV. Find out what type. Does he go RVing often? Probe! Probe!

Do not interrogate or badger. It's possible you'll have to work with a salesperson with whom you've had an active encounter. He may be just a hard-working professional who doesn't know very much about RVs. Your neighborhood dealer may be the best to buy from, but you may have to make all the decisions without his help. Keep in mind that RV salespeople also have bad days. Customers who aren't friendly or courteous

Probe!
But watch out
for sharp teeth.

may set a mood that carries through to the final sale. Since you have control, you don't need to be nasty. Just do your thing by asking those five questions.

What about questions relating to tow vehicles?

Every RV salesperson should know about towing vehicles. I know one RV salesperson who still looks at the GVWR (Gross Vehicle Weight Rating) on the door pillar of the truck to tell his customers how heavy a trailer they can tow. The towing vehicle's GVWR, of course, does not tell you its trailer-towing capacity. There is absolutely no excuse for an RV salesperson not having towing specs at his fingertips. Do not forgive any absence of this knowledge or the inability to provide the information. Life has been too easy for these so-called professionals. It's time for that to change.

Towing a motorized vehicle behind a motor home is more technically demanding than towing a trailer. If a mistake is made in choosing the right vehicle, the cost can be heavy. If the RV salesperson has information about dinghy towing in writing, give him an A$^+$. If the information is verbal, double check it.

Under no condition accept a *"Sure, it can pull this without a problem,"* or *"Sure, this can be pulled without a problem."* Watching a salesperson's lips move about towing specs is tantamount to asking for disaster. All the information you need is in the vehicle manufacturer's towing guide — whether a truck or a car.

Another concern is that the towing specifications from vehicle manufacturers are always liberal. Since there is big competition among pickup truck lines, manufacturers know they are going to lose sales if they can't say their trucks will pull enough to satisfy the RVer. Since they're in business to sell what they build, you can bet they'll give you the highest towing

Don't worry, your truck will pull anything on this lot.

capacity they can justify. If an RV or truck salesperson says you can easily exceed the towing limit shown in the specification sheet, don't trust him with your money. Although some RVers do seem to get by exceeding these towing limits, the odds of premature wear and accidents are stacked against them. I've seen a half-ton truck pulling a 12,000-pound fifth wheel, and I don't ever want to be behind the wheel of such an overburdened vehicle. Towing guides are a must, and a maximum towing limit is absolutely a maximum.

Should I ask about competitor's brands?

If you really want to shake up a salesperson, ask him to compare his RVs to a competitor's brands. Most salespeople hate talking about the competition. They'll say they don't like knocking the other guy. You come back with, *"Don't knock it, just tell me the facts."* Wait for the response. Smoothy will usually dump you fast, but a good salesperson will hang in there.

To know about the competition is difficult for the RV salesperson who already has a hard time understanding about his own brands. He may have to take a day off to visit an RV show or another dealership. Unless he's forced into it, he'll never do it.

If the salesperson tries to give a comparison presentation but can't seem to get it together, put the competitor's brochure on the RV's table next to his brochure. Compare construction features — especially roof, frame, and suspension. This is also a good opportunity to compare optional equipment. Make the salesperson work with you on the differences. Don't forget to make notes on the brochures. If you do this with every dealer you visit, you'll have a wealth of information at your fingertips.

Finding out what the competition has to offer can be very scary to a salesperson.

Can you give me an example of what I can ask and what I should get for an answer?

Sure. Here are five simple questions and expected responses (ER). Keep in mind, however, that most of the answers should be quite extensive.

Q. How much does it weigh?

ER: The salesperson should show you the GVWR on the RV or in the brochure. If he throws out a figure without looking at the brochure or spec tag on the RV, you can almost bet he's guessing. If he goes for the gross dry weight or gross wet weight, push the issue. Ask for the maximum weight you'll be towing. Stand your ground. Don't settle for figures rolling off the tongue. If this information is not accurately given, put a 1 on this salesperson's business card (on a score of 1 to 10 with 10 being the best).

Q. What size tow vehicle do I need?

ER: The answer to this one should be given to you carefully and with some thoughtfulness. The salesperson should find your needs before he makes a recommendation. He should pull out a towing guide and explain how it works in conjunction with the trailer specifications. This is, of course, a good time for him to take you to his office and attempt a trial close. Give him credit for trying — after all, that's his job.

Q. How is it insulated?

ER: With this question you should get more than a brochure response. If the salesperson is a professional, a question like this will give him a chance to show his stuff. He should get into R values and types of insulation. He should talk about the differences between aluminum and fiberglass as insulators. He should talk about the roof material and structure, and explain the overall R-value. ('R value' is explained in the full version of *The Language of RVing*, which is the glossary section in *The RV Ratings Guide CD*.)

Q. Do I need storm windows?

ER: When you ask this question, you'll get more opinions than good answers. To answer this question correctly, the salesperson should ask you some very pertinent questions before he goes overboard with the technical stuff. After all, you may simply want to know if you need storm windows. He should talk about use, window size, condensation, and the overall insulation factor.

Q. How does this brand rate against a _____?

ER: Expect specifics on construction and interior quality. He should always use the real model for his argument. If he asks you where you saw the brand, it's okay to tell him. If he asks you about the price, don't tell him. The question should not allow him to go on a fishing expedition. You simply want accurate answers so you can make an intelligent buying decision. Tell him that if he wants your business he'll have to earn it — the old fashioned way.

Don't leave home in the dark...

Always take a flashlight, a notepad, and 5 questions.

Put in an RV cam and it'll work fine. I'll even deduct the cost from the trailer price.

I could hardly believe this one myself. I heard it with my own ears. The truck was rated to pull just under 3,000 pounds less than the GVWR of the fifth wheel travel trailer. To make matters worse, the truck was a short bed and couldn't make a legal turn without the front of the fifth wheel hitting the cab. In this case, Smoothy knew exactly what he was doing.

Chapter 17

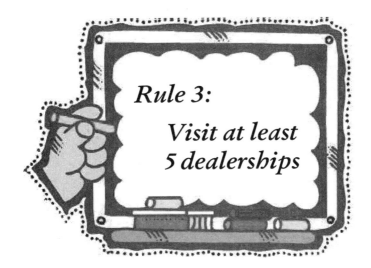

Rule 3:

*Visit at least
5 dealerships*

During your initial visits to the dealerships, you should make decisions on type, size, and quality. You'll need at least five dealers for this input. You'll need to collect retail prices and trade allowances if you have a trade-in. Write the retail price and the trade allowance in the brochure for future study. And, of course, you'll collect copies of MSRP sheets which you'll fasten to the appropriate brochures.

Don't be led by the nose. Demand facts. No facts, no talky. You must learn to control the buying decision from the very beginning. Be friendly, be firm.

Always keep in mind that your initial visits are to collect information. Expect a Smoothy to drop you fast if he senses you are on a research mission. Good salespeople, however, will take your name, address, and telephone number and offer to help you get the information you need.

Beware of dealerships that lock all RVs. Reasons for this policy are generally not valid. At the very least, expect some display models to be open. A closed lot usually indicates high pressure (and high profit) selling techniques. Keeping all RVs locked has been advocated by some sales-motivation experts as a device for controlled qualifying and presentations. Closed

RVs have merits, but those merits do not generally benefit the consumer.

Visit the dealership's service area even if you do it on your own. Stand back and observe the technicians at work. Try to get a sense of their proficiency. Give the service department at least five minutes of your time.

Try to eavesdrop on the salespeople. You'll be surprised at what you hear. Listening to RV salespeople talk with prospects will give you an idea of what you'll be facing.

It's fun if you do it right.

What should I say when I first walk into an RV dealership?

Your first approach is very important. I recommend calling the dealership first and talking to more than one salesperson. Ask pertinent questions about the dealership and its brands. Stay away from the technical stuff on the phone. If you feel comfortable with a particular salesperson, you may want to make an appointment. Keep in mind, however, that Smoothies are very good on the phone. Their objective is to get you to their desk. They know that most incoming telephone calls are gold-lined.

If a salesperson knows how to use the phone for prospecting, he'll get your name and number almost immediately. He'll find a reason for

Hi! I'm Sue and I'm looking for an RV, but I don't know what kind I want or how much I should be paying. I am going to buy in about two months. I need a lot of questions answered because I read this book that said...

calling you back. Expect aggressiveness. It's a sign of sales professionalism. Expect him to pump you for the 'urgency' factor. If you get an obvious nitwit or a Smoothy, don't give any information. If the reception is good after you tell him or her about your basic needs, you may want to find out the salesperson's working schedule and plan your visit accordingly.

Whether you talk on the phone or in person, keep the impression going that you are a serious buyer. Never say, *"I'm just shopping,"* or *"I'm going to buy when I find the right RV."* Both of these statements do the wrong things. If you say "shopping", you either turn the salesperson off or get him into a fast qualifying mode. If you say "buying", you are pushing a button for the sale today. Those in the business know that 'hot' buyers are itchy to hit the road. They also know that if these hot-to-trot prospects leave the lot, they'll probably never be seen again because they'll get caught at the competition. RVers who mention buying will be given fast tours, hit hard with trial closes, and get turned before they leave the lot. The pressure will be heavy. Be serious about buying, but try, *"I'm going to buy an RV in the near future."* This honest approach might get you that professional salesperson who will be willing to work with you.

Hello Sue, this is Bill at First Place RV. I wanted to let you know the RV you liked so much was put on special this month. If you can come in today, I think I can arrange...

What will an MSRP sheet really tell me?

A genuine MSRP (Manufacturer's Suggested Retail Price) sheet and a good brochure will tell you almost everything available in print about a particular model. You need both if you want to make a good purchase. Be sure you include a copy of the MSRP sheet in the brochure of any brand you may consider.

Study the drawing below. Notice the standard equipment column on the left. The same equipment will be listed in the brochure for every model of the same brand. Don't get confused between models. What is standard on one model may not be standard on another. Most manufacturers will designate a model change if the standard equipment changes. Standard

---

MANUFACTURER'S SUGGESTED RETAIL PRICE

DEALER	MANUFACTURING PLANT	INVOICE #
ADDRESS	BRAND MODEL COLOR	YEAR
VEHICLE SERIAL NUMBER	DATE OF MANUFACTURE	

THE FOLLOWING ITEMS ARE STANDARD ON THIS MODEL AT NO EXTRA CHARGE	MANUFACTURER'S SUGGESTED RETAIL PRICE OF THIS MODEL: $ _____
	OPTIONAL EQUIPMENT INSTALLED ON THIS VEHICLE BY MANUFACTURER OPTION # DESCRIPTION
	OPTIONS SUBTOTAL _____ VEHICLE TOTAL DESTINATION CHARGE _____ DEALER PREP _____ OTHER _____ TOTAL AMOUNT $ _____

equipment cannot usually be removed for special orders. Most good manufacturers will show a base price for each model. This base MSRP includes all the standard equipment. It does not include optional equipment.

On the right side of the sheet you will find a list of optional equipment installed by the manufacturer. A dealer can change the optional equipment for stock items or special orders. Some manufacturers have 'standard runs' that include specific optional equipment unless a request is received from a dealer for an addition or deletion. For example: a standard run may include a spare tire, but a dealer who wants a 'special' for a show or promotion could exclude the spare from a number of units. Most buyers would not notice the omission when comparing prices with a competitor. You must, therefore, be very careful when comparing optional equipment.

Honey, look here. The man said that the bypass valve was optional but here it is on the standard equipment list. I think he was trying to cheat us.

An easy way to overcome manipulation of optional equipment is to look at the box shown as 'options subtotal'. Any difference in the list will be reflected in the dollar figure in this box. Genuine MSRP sheets are designed so you can get a consistent value for the 'vehicle total' amount. This is the figure you must compare when working with two or more dealers for the same model.

You can't do much about the destination charge unless it's inflated, but watch out for the "dealer prep." This is usually a bonus amount for the dealer. Disregard it in all computations unless something special has been done to the RV at the dealership. If so, demand to know what was done and find out whether it's an excuse to inflate the figure.

The vehicle total price is very important for negotiations when buy-day arrives. It will tell you how much to expect as an allowance for a trade-in or how much you should receive as a discount. The vehicle total figure is based on a multiplying factor from manufacturing cost figures. It is possible for the multiplying factor to change from plant to plant or to adjust for inflation and other costs. Usually, however, variations in this figure are negligible.

You should also note that the manufacturing plant is shown on the MSRP sheet. The location of the plant will tell you if the transportation charge is legitimate. (Charge should be $1 per mile **maximum**.)

Getting a genuine MSRP sheet is paramount. Most are two colors. Good manufacturers produce one computer-generated two-color MSRP sheet for each motor home or travel trailer built. Do not negotiate with any dealer who refuses to give you a copy of the MSRP sheet or order form with list prices. You can make adequate comparisons with either one.

How do I compare one RV brand with another — especially if I decide to go used?

To buy a used RV, you'll need to visit at least five dealerships to get a good feel for brand and floor plan availability. You'll have to leave your telephone number with any salesperson interested in future business. Most will use a card filing system to keep in touch. The good salespeople will call you as soon as anything comes in that fits your basic requirements. Most, however, will never call you.

If you are considering an RV no older than five years, you should compare with new models. Begin by using MSRP sheets and advertised prices as a basis for the real value of the purchase. Keep brochures and MSRP sheets just as if you were going to buy new. I can't begin to tell you the number of RVers who have paid as much (and sometimes more) for a used RV as a new one.

Smoothy knows how to apply the pressure on an exceptional used RV. He will say, *"There's not another one exactly like it anywhere."* He'll be right, of course. Every used RV is unique because of the wear and tear factor. This doesn't mean, however, that you should rush into buying the first decent used RV you find. Extensive shopping is still a priority. The old adage 'there's always another fish' applies as much to RVs as to anything else. Don't let Smoothy hook you.

If you decide to buy an RV over five years old, go primarily by brand and condition. Quality should be the big priority. Later on we'll get into appraising — something you'll want to learn.

When buying used, you'll compare prices and condition through your notes. Don't expect to remember everything.

Send us *The RV Ratings Guide* CD!

Most of us remember three things — then we're lost. You may do better than the average, but you'll save a lot of money by using pencil and paper.

There's a danger in trusting a salesperson's opinion on used RVs because the profits are usually larger than with new. After you look at twenty or thirty used RVs, you're almost ready for anything that looks good. Don't be fooled into accepting too many compromises.

How about buying from a private party?

You can get a very good buy from a private party, but use the same techniques as when buying from a dealer. Do the dealer route first. After you get past a number of dealers, you may be interested in starting a search for a private party sale; but consider the following:

1) Many of these sellers have had plenty of experience handling people, they have a sense of the market, and they know that many buyers don't trust dealers.

2) When you buy from an individual, you have almost no recourse once you pay. It's usually a pure 'buyer beware' situation.

3) The private party is usually in love with the RV even if they don't know its real condition and value. They get their figures from the newspaper or from the asking price of the local dealer.

I've seen as many people get ripped off by private owners as by dealers. If you don't follow the same basic procedure as buying from a dealer, your dollars will be in mortal danger.

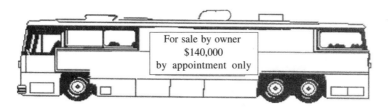

This simple statement, and many variations thereof, has moved enough RVs off the sales lots to circle the globe. We have, unfortunately, a learned reflex of listening more intently when we hear the words *save*, *discount*, or *special*. Smoothy has also learned to use these words after he gets a buying signal from you. You say *"This is nice,"* and he'll say something with the words *discount*, *save*, or *special*. Listen for them — but don't bite!

Chapter 18

Rule 4:

Don't trust the salesperson until he or she earns it.

I do not wish to imply that the bulk of RV salespeople are not trustworthy. To the contrary, most RV salespeople want to give you good service while making a reasonable living. It's the American way. Of all the salespeople I've met, most of them want to be considered good, solid citizens.

As you begin your search, you should listen carefully to each salesperson. Be aware that he or she is trying hard to get your trust. Getting trust quickly is the "in thing" for RV dealerships. RV salespeople are encouraged to qualify, present, and close as quickly as possible. Their pay depends upon the close. They learn manipulative techniques to get you to that point. Even the most conscientious salesperson will manipulate a prospect. It's his duty. It's what the boss demands of him. The problem, however, is that manipulation destroys trust.

When you cut off any chance of closing today, most salespeople will lose interest. It's a natural state of the business. Don't write a salesperson off just because he or she won't spend hours with you on your search. Don't be totally unfair.

You should not feel obligated to ask for a particular salesperson on a second or third visit. Unless you feel strongly inclined, take whoever comes along. If the salesperson asks if you've been working with someone else, say, *"I've been talking to _____ , but you're okay with me."* Leave it there. They'll work it out.

The value of information collected from salespeople depends upon the accuracy — and honesty — of their spoken words. Make notes, then rate each salesperson on a scale of 1 to 10 — just like you would an RV. This rating will come in handy when you're ready to deal seriously.

How do RV salespeople qualify a buyer?

Each salesperson qualifies differently. The way they're supposed to do it is to ask you some 'when', 'what', and 'how' questions upfront. Most aren't that good at it. They generally stumble through the process by looking at the way you're dressed, the condition of the vehicle you're driving, or by what

The 'quick' qualifier . . .

misuses the system.

you incidentally tell them. Some don't qualify until they get into a presentation — if they get that far. A few will be precise. They are the professionals. You'll get a sense they've had some sales experience even if they don't know much about RVs.

Expect to be looked over even if not looked at. A real Smoothy will push hard for information by the time you get to the first RV. Somehow he'll find out if there's an urgency and then he'll go for your budget. His mind will be working fast. He may give you ten minutes if there's a chance that you're a 'hot' prospect.

Smoothy is always looking for a 'lay-down'. He wants the ones he can manipulate. He knows that 3 out of 10 RV buyers are 'easy-sells'. If you find yourself being dumped within fifteen minutes, you may have found a Smoothy — and he may have found that you are too tough.

If the salesperson sticks with you after you've convinced him you're a serious buyer, expect the qualifying to continue.

You should get probing questions about lifestyle and past preferences in RVs. Under no circumstances give your social security number or credit information at this time.

What is a trial close?

A trial close is the salesperson's test of your resistance to closing (signing the contract). For example, you say, *"I like it,"* and he immediately pushes the urgency issue. He may even try to get you to the office to work on the figures. A professional salesperson will look for buying signals, so you must avoid offhand remarks about exceptional features. Some RV buyers get so emotional that the buying signals never stop.

Buying signals will stop a good presentation. When the signal is given, a salesperson will probably try to get you into a closing situation. When it doesn't work, he'll start over but the presentation might lose something in the meantime. If you nod too many times, he'll make a move like, *"Would $300 a month be about right?"* or *"Let's see what we can work out in figures."* Trial closes are exciting for a professional salesperson because it's a test of qualifying, gaining trust, and manipulation. It's all designed to get you to the desk.

What is a 'turn'?

A 'turn' is a technique of passing you to another salesperson or the sales manager. This procedure is often required at auto dealerships and has found its way into many RV dealerships. In many ways, it's required because of weaknesses in the system. If the salesperson has good qualifying and follow-up techniques, the turn shouldn't be necessary.

Because RV selling often lacks professionalism, you may find the turn an interesting aspect of your RV shopping. Be aware that the 'turn' is often made to another salesperson with a false title. Usually this is obvious. If the 'turn' is to a real sales manager, be cordial — get as much information as you can. The sales manager is often the most informed person on the staff.

When you've had enough, emphasize that you must leave. Don't get caught with flapping lips. Keep the plan going.

Before you go, I'd like to have you meet our sales manager.

When and how do I walk out gracefully?

Keep it simple! *"I have to go,"* works fine. Don't put a time limit too early into the session. If the salesperson is getting into a presentation, take advantage of it. Don't rush off. Get all you can when you can.

A good salesperson will not let you go until you make a trip to the office. *"Let's load you down with brochures,"* is a statement that should work for him. When in the office, he might try, *"While you're here, how about some figures?"* You'll find it hard to stay away from the salesperson's desk. If you find yourself there, spend time with the brochures. Watch out for hard-sell tactics. Because every salesperson should be proficient in getting you to his desk, you have to be ready to apply the brakes. Since most salespeople won't give you much for figures if you aren't buying today, take your brochure and run.

Don't forget . . .

these things
could happen to
you.

When Smoothy said this, he didn't know whether it was true or not. He said it because it sounded like the right thing to say to overcome an objection. If you want to have fun playing a detective, look the salesperson in the face and ask a couple of those prepared questions when a statement of this nature is made. The answers should help you determine if this person is worth your time.

Chapter 19

Rule 5:

Expect a good presentation of each RV shown.

A presentation is an exposure of the features and benefits of a product or service. A good RV salesperson will take you through a presentation in a manner adjusted in time and intensity to your needs.

Always ask for a brochure before the presentation begins. By now you know that the brochure is important, but from now on you're going to learn that it's an indispensable tool for a good buy.

If the salesperson begins by making an organized presentation, let him lead. If the presentation is poorly performed, take over — lead the way by asking questions. Either way, make notes in the brochure of the RV's interesting features and the prices quoted.

A good presentation will include positive statements about the features (i.e. the rubber roof, the enclosed propane bottles, the special suspension) and statements about the benefit of those features (example: *"The rubber roof's insulation and noise reduction abilities will make living in the RV more comfortable."*). Lazy salespeople won't do this because it takes rehearsing and study.

The presentation should be considered your reward for visiting a dealership. Do not accept a simple tour of the inventory. If explanations are not given and questions are not completely answered, you should wipe the salesperson from your list of candidates for buy-day.

Nice wood!

In case you have to control the presentation, you should have an organized plan. Prepare to lead the salesperson around the RV while asking about construction features. Prepare questions about the roof. Dress casually so that you can easily study the suspension. Have questions ready about the axles, rails, and tires. You will, in actuality, be conducting an appraisal of the RV—a subject covered in section 2.

Inside, you will check the galley (kitchen) first then the bathroom and the bedroom. Look at the cabinetry and the fixtures. Study the cabinet cuts. Drawers are very important. Quality of material and workmanship must be noted. Look into corners and under cushions. When you get to the bathroom, plan on spending a few minutes studying the seams around the shower. Is it a real shower (fiberglass or ABS walls) or an imitation shower (vinyl walls)? If you plan on using the shower often, you won't want anything

A touch tight!

It may be too short.

except a high quality wraparound stall. If you spend most of your inspection time in the galley and bathroom, you'll soon begin to get the big picture of overall quality.

Whether the salesperson leads or you lead, don't get shortchanged. A presentation, a brochure, and brands printout from *The RV Ratings Guide CD* are requirements for a good buying decision.

How do I ask for a presentation?

Be bold! An organized presentation is the essence of the sales process. Whether or not a salesperson can properly qualify or close, he must be able to intelligently talk about the product. *"Will you tell me about this brand?"* should be enough to get a presentation going. Of my students who have gone on a serious shopping campaigns, less than 10% have been able to get a good presentation. They report having to lead the salesperson by asking pertinent questions. Because of these low percentages, you'll have to get what you can when you can.

If you come across an experienced salesperson, allow him or her to go through the complete presentation with minimum interruptions. Don't give buying signals. Keep busy taking notes. A good salesperson likes the attention given by a prospect. If he tries to rush through the presentation, you may have to question him to slow him down.

May I get a presentation, please?

What is a good RV presentation?

A good presentation is well practiced — just like staging a show. If the presenter is skillful, he'll get into the details smoothly. In the first place, he'll be sure that a complete presentation is made only on an RV in which you have interest. I recommend that an RV salesperson have two presentations ready: a shopper presentation and a buyer presentation.

The shopper presentation, if performed correctly, will get into particulars about the manufacturer, the brand, and general construction. On an RV, this should take about five minutes. It will cover all points in an organized manner. The presenter should begin near the front where you can see the name and the profile as he points to important structural and design characteristics. He'll then take you inside where he'll talk about features and benefits distinct to the brand — not the particular model. After about five minutes, he should encourage you to ask questions.

A good presenter will know when to stop talking and begin looking for buying signals. If the interest in the particular RV is genuine, he may ask you if you have the time for a complete presentation. If you indicate you don't have the time, a good salesperson will immediately try to get an appointment. If rapport has been established, you will probably go for this approach.

Let me show you the new features with benefits.

If you show serious interest in a particular RV or brand, a professional salesperson will attempt to take you through a complete buyer presentation. With RVs this takes between twenty and thirty minutes. If the presentation is too short, something will have been left out. If it's too long, you will get weary and the salesperson will feel rushed to get you into a closing situation. An effective buyer presentation begins with qualifying. If you are primarily destined for a motor home, a complete presentation on a travel trailer would be a waste of time.

Listen carefully to the presenter. If he starts talking too fast, slow him down so you don't miss anything. Keep your spouse with you. Both of you must give the presenter full attention. This is simple courtesy. A presentation of any product is a serious act.

After the presentation, take a moment to go over your notes with the salesperson. He might have valuable insights that are relevant and helpful. If he's been in RV sales for over five years, his comments should have some value.

How do I check out an RV on my own?

Because of the difficulty of getting a good presentation on an RV, you're going to be prepared to check it out all by yourself. It's quite easy and can be fun. In most cases, you should ask the salesperson for permission. If you do it right, he'll get the point and leave you alone.

You'll need your brochure in hand. Don't inspect an RV without it. A well-designed brochure will illustrate every feature the manufacturer can muster (who should know better than the manufacturer?). The manufacturers have spent hundreds of hours and thousands of dollars to put this booklet into

Notice the floor is attached to the frame every four inches so you won't feel the road bumps in your feet.

your hand. They've given you their building secrets. They've dissected the competition to make their product's distinguishing features stand out. Even with all this work, most brochures will go to waste. Yours won't. You're going to use it as a guide to check out the real product.

There should be two or three pages in the brochure that cover construction features. Some will even get into the techniques and philosophy of building. This information is worth its weight in gold. The task at hand is for you to compare these illustrations and specifications with those you see in the real model.

During your walkabout, as discussed in section 2, look for interesting features and deficiencies. Think of it as competition in a game or a sport. You are out to win. You're out to overpower the glitter makers for your dollars and your future. Whether you are with a salesperson or alone, you will need to fight for control. You will need to lift, poke, touch, and smell. If you make it a habit, it will stay with you every time you enter an RV. When you sit at home, you'll remember things in the same order as when you inspected the real thing. You'll soon begin to feel confident that your 5-year plan will be more than a dream — it will be a vision of your adventures to come.

This is the state-of-the-art in RVs.
It has the best in structure and insulation.

This statement was made by a salesperson who knew the RV being shown was below entry level. It was being shown to a little old lady who wanted to live alone on relatives' property.

Smoothy is quick to judge the knowledge and naivete of the prospect. His words are his weapons when he moves in for the kill. Like a military tank, Smoothy has but one purpose.

Chapter 20

Rule 6:

Go for
the quality!

It is important to remember that quality and brand are not necessarily synonymous. Many brands have had severe changes in building characteristics because the brand name changed ownership. Some of these brands have been reduced in quality. Some have been upgraded. When looking for a new RV, you can usually judge brands, like wines, as being consistent only for a particular year. If looking for used, you'll have to be very careful.

At this point you should be ready to choose a brand and an alternate. You should have established a budget and know which brands will fit that budget. If you need to adjust your budget later, you may have to switch from new to used. If you go used, it might be practical to consider from three to five brands. All the knowledge and notes you have collected will be very important if you go this route.

The average RV buyer ignores brands because he's been told that the differences are minor. The RV industry has been careful not to be critical of the competition because every manufacturer knows how vulnerable its own brands are. RV

manufacturing is profitable because of consumer ignorance —
and some manufacturers want to keep it that way.

You should, of course, study *The RV Ratings Guide CD*. It
will give you the ratings of each model of most brands. As you
get into the process, keep an open mind. It's easy to get caught
in glitter and floor plan. It's easy to rationalize buying lower
quality. It's easy to accept pleasing yourself, or another, in spite
of the facts. Your goal should be to hit the road with your RV
as a good investment — not just an expenditure.

How do I know that the brand is good?

By now you should know the importance of good presentations and of your own appraisals. If you follow the first six
rules of this book, you will eliminate 50% of the brands on the
market.

I like to have my students start their appraisals with the roof
and the galley. By checking the roof for quality of workmanship
and materials, you'll get a good picture of what's under the skin.
If you see flaws on the exterior, especially the roof, you can bet

*The RV Ratings Guide CD
shows that it's rated a 70 when
used for vacations.*

there are even more deficiencies you can't see without taking the RV apart.

We have a sign in our conference room that says, *"The manufacturer who can't build a good galley can't build a good RV."* This statement has been reinforced time and time again by data and comments put into our computer's memory banks. There is no question at RV Consumer Group that if the galley is designed for vacation use, the rest of the RV is built for vacation use. This doesn't mean the quality is poor; it means the quality is adequate for vacation use — not snowbirding or fulltiming. This difference is important.

Long ago I discounted the flat one-piece aluminum roof as being so deficient in long-life qualities that I downgrade every RV with this type of roof. Whether the aluminum has no backing or hardbacking makes little difference to me. The philosophy of any manufacturer who uses this roof material is always in question. They know this type of material is not forgiving of workmanship or maintenance deficiencies. They know that for a few bucks more they can do better. They also know that 75% of the RV buying public is ignorant of this roof's tendency to leak. It's all tied up in the big game of marketing and profit.

So in the short of it, you can't know that a brand is good beyond the model year on which you're working. There is absolutely no sure way of knowing if a particular unit is good even though the brand's rating is high. Lemons happen, and some factories produce more lemons than others. Choosing a manufacturer who has a reputation for sloppy workmanship means more chances of buying a lemon. By going for quality in workmanship you're betting that what was a consistently good brand in the past will be a good brand today.

How far down do I settle for less?

It all gets down to bravery. If you feel secure in risking thousands of dollars on looks, go for whatever looks good to you. If, however, you buy an RV rated below 60 in *The RV Ratings Guide* CD, I think you are asking for lots of frustration when you hit the road.

Don't gamble...

on quality!

I personally don't want to be bothered by junk at my stage of life. I don't need a gold-plated RV, but I want substance. I've found out there's rarely a reason to drop in quality.

What do I say to a relative or friend who has one of *those?*

Having a neighbor, relative, or friend show up with an RV that you have learned is not of acceptable quality puts you in a tough spot. Once they find out that you're in the upper 10% of the world in RV knowledge (which you will be by the time you finish this book) they will, sooner or later, ask for your opinion. Because almost everyone is defensive of their actions when it comes to spending money, even if they complain, watch out. If you want to keep these people as friends, you better say little. Show them you care by buying them a copy of this book. They might believe me quicker than they'll believe you. Absolutely do not bring up the issue. Don't lose friendship to prove a point.

Every RVer has the responsibility of spreading information about RVing. To get the point across, use short phrases like:

▸ *"All RVs are not created equal."*
▸ *"A good RV begins with a good roof and superb galley."*
▸ *"RVs should last twenty years without major failure."*

When you spread this kind of information, you'll sleep well knowing you have given your friends insights toward making the right choices.

This is the best buy for the money!

Smoothy said this about a brand rated below 60 in *The RV Ratings Guide CD*. Smoothy says it so often in one way or another that it sounds convincing. There's no hesitation, eye shifting, or stammer. He waits for a buying signal — then POW!

Smoothy is an expert at shifting gears. He'll work the trust game. He'll play the *take it or leave it* game. If he sees a weakness, he might go for the throat almost immediately.

Chapter 21

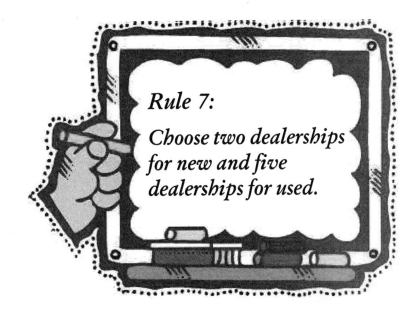

Rule 7:

Choose two dealerships for new and five dealerships for used.

The smart RV buyer begins with the local dealerships and gives those dealerships the benefit of the doubt. You, as a smart RV buyer, will communicate by visits and by phone. You will get to know the management. If, however, the dealership does not have acceptable brands, you will drop it like a hot potato.

Beware of dealerships that are considered regional discount houses. Although these dealerships usually have some good brands, they also have hot-shot salespeople. Regional discount houses work beyond their communities. They bring buyers in — and close them today. You will probably have a tough time getting good information at an RV discount house.

By now you should have made your decision on type, size, and price range. You should be working hard on brand and floor plan. Choosing dealerships and salespeople with whom you can work is very important at this time. You will need rapport with the salesperson if you want to get the best deal possible. A good salesperson will represent the dealership while caring about your needs.

If you are buying used, be sure you understand the complications and techniques we are discussing in this section. Because any dealer can take in any type, size, brand, or floor plan as a trade, you need to be listed with as many dealerships as practical. Whether you buy new or used, what you're after is the best RV you can buy for the money you have budgeted.

Is it right to work one dealership against the other?

Oh yes! It's an old game of skirmishes. They work you — you work them. Even though you have the advantage, they have the record for winning. They are not, of course, going to win this battle. By now, you understand the importance of control and direction. You're going to keep your eye on the 5-year plan as you control visits, time, and the pen. If you get out of control, Smoothy will win — and you know it.

By now you have a file full of brochures and accurate figures from the five dealerships you've been visiting. You have already chosen type and size and are narrowing it to two brands. You have a close idea of your floor plan, and you'll have worked your budget to within 10%. By this time you'll be loaded with copies of MSRP sheets and worksheets for brands and models you are considering. You'll have your brands printout from *The RV Ratings Guide CD* under your arm. You have the power in your hands to take control of buy-day.

As you visit one of the two dealerships you've chosen for the buy, you may or may not have chosen the person with whom you'll negotiate. This is not really important unless you've found that exceptional salesperson. Since you probably know exactly what you're after, the visits to the dealerships from now on are primarily to get the final figures for study.

Tell the salesperson your timetable. Tell him that you're making a decision soon and that he's competing with another dealer. Do not, and I repeat, do not tell the salesperson which other dealership you are considering. If the salesperson knows the other dealership's sales philosophy, he'll know how to work you. Keep him guessing. Tell him what brand and model you're considering. If it requires a special order, you'll need to get accurate specifics at this time. Find out the location of the manufacturing plant. (It should be on the MSRP sheet, but double check anyway.)

On this last visit before you decide which dealer to try, you may want to get any final advice the salesperson can give. Listen intently. If he thinks you're still wavering, he'll work hard to get your trust. A salesperson may hold back giving advice if he thinks the prospect is inflexible. Even though he may know something you don't about other models or equipment, he may be reluctant to advise you for fear of losing whatever he has going. Show your interest by listening. It's your last chance before buy-day.

The ball game changes a bit if you're going for used. With used you have to be ready to deal the day you look. Like new, however, you should know what you want and what compromises you're willing to make. The big difference will be that you can't order another just like it.

If you get excited over a used RV, try for a 3-day $100 refundable hold. This will give you time to check further and to think about it. The value of a hold, however, depends much on the dealership. Some dealerships will limit holds to a shorter time and may require a firmer commitment. The dealer's reputation for honoring a hold is very important when buying used. You need to be aware that some dealers use the hold to push the next prospect on the same vehicle for a quick sale at a higher profit.

Whether buying new or used, be honest about your time-table and needs. Work hard at getting the salesperson excited about working with you on the purchase. If the salesperson says, *"I'll beat anybody's price,"* you know you are beginning to get control of buy-day.

What about those telephone calls?

You'll be kept busy on the phone. Be polite, be brief, be honest, and don't blab! Set a maximum of ten minutes for any call. Make the salesperson call back if necessary. If you have a real Smoothy, he'll promise you anything to get you to his desk. Some salespeople aren't good on the phone. Some are gabby — don't waste your time with these. Use the telephone to your advantage by qualifying the salesperson. It's a great reverse play. If you come to the conclusion that you don't want a particular salesperson to call again, say so. If you've made up your mind to buy from another dealer, be honest and say so. By being honest, you might get some fascinating figures.

Yes, I'm looking at the inventory right now. We have exactly what you want.

If you promise to go to the dealership for any reason, don't make an appointment unless you intend to keep it. A good salesperson will work his/her butt off for a forthright buyer. I've seen some tremendous deals because the salesperson worked the sales manager into going for less profit.

What do I do with the salesperson who turns me off at a dealership that otherwise seems good?

Call the dealership until you find a salesperson with whom you think you can work. Make an appointment. If seen by the other salesperson, acknowledge only with a slight nod or smile. Do not encourage the other salesperson to interfere. Snub him if necessary. If queried by the new salesperson about the other, simply say, *"You're doing fine."* Do not get involved in a discussion on commission splits or say anything negative about the other salesperson. Let them hash it out.

What do you mean you don't want me as your salesperson? I'm the only one here that knows anything!

I'll beat anybody's price!

This is probably one of the few things you should be happy to hear Smoothy say. It opens the door for a discussion of prices. It gives you a chance to pin him down and make him sweat.

Don't let Smoothy forget that he said those four **big** words.

Chapter 22

Rule 8:

Have all your facts on paper.

You can't make a good buy without some information on paper. The more you have, the stronger your chances of getting within 2% of the best deal possible. Most people ignore collecting information because it takes time and effort. I learned over a 40-year span that savings in time and money were proportional to the habit of collecting information at each step of the way. That's the way it works for me, and it can do the same for you.

When you visit a dealership, you should have plenty of ammunition in a closed folder or small case. You should have a brochure for every RV you are considering. You should have the MSRP (Manufacturer's Suggested Retail Price) sheet if new or the average book retail if used. You should have *The RV Ratings Guide* CD's highway control, reliability, and value ratings marked in bold numbers on the cover of every brochure.

If you have a trade, know the appraisal book wholesale and retail figures. When you know the ACV (Actual Cash Value) of your trade, you can figure how much to expect as an allowance on another RV. Most RV buyers lose money because they don't know how to figure their trade into the deal.

There is nothing that will keep a salesperson on his or her toes like a buyer loaded for bear. A good salesperson will accept it as a challenge — knowing the profit may be minimal but the prize is still worth going after. When you have the information in hand, you will gain respect — and you will deserve it.

How do I get realistic used RV values?

If you are buying used, have a trade-in, or are trying to figure depreciation factors for the brand you are considering, you will need to use two appraisal books — *N.A.D.A.* and *Kelley Blue Book*. You can usually find these books at the library, bank, credit union, or on the Internet. I recommend averaging from both books since both use nationwide subscriber input to determine the values.

Most dealers use both books. Smart salespeople know how to use appraisal books to their advantage. For example: If the customer asks to see the book value on an RV being considered, the salesperson will show the book with the highest value. Of course, he will do the opposite for trade-ins. Some dealers also use outdated books to their advantage. Always check the months and year on the book cover. Ask for copies of the applicable pages. If you can't get copies, make notes of the values. Dealers make plenty of money on trades because most RV buyers are ignorant of trade values. I have seen hundreds of RV buyers make seemingly good deals until further checking showed the trade was practically given away. Knowing the value of your trade will save you  thousands of dollars — an incentive that should make you work harder for buy-day.

An appraisal book will give you the following data: 1) the original MSRP base price (suggested list when new), 2) the used wholesale, 3) the used retail, 4) optional equipment values, and 5) a mileage schedule for motor homes. You will need all five of these values. Keep in mind that optional equipment values are overrated by the dealer when selling and underrated when figuring trade-in allowances. Optional equipment does not include any item that is standard equipment when new. If you average the figures from both books, you should have a good beginning for ACV. You will also need to add or subtract for the condition and for any reduced demand of a particular type, model, or floor plan in your section of the country. I recommend no more than 20% for pluses, but there's no limit on negatives.

Most salespeople cannot appraise accurately. For this reason, you may find big variations in used values among dealers. We have found great used RV values at dealerships because a trade was brought in low. On the other side of the picture, you'll find many used RV prices out-of-sight because the dealer allowed too much. The unlucky buyer is the one who thinks all prices are fair. You don't. Your plan is to buy low and trade high.

How important is the warranty?

A warranty is very important because it separates the good, well-established manufacturers from all others. Without warranty facts in your hand, you don't know what the warranty is. Some manufacturers — like Fleetwood, Winnebago, Carriage, and Holiday Rambler — will furnish complete warranty details on request. Get them and study them.

Smaller manufacturers may have a good warranty on their products if you can find a service center to do the work. These details have to be considered. If you buy from one of these smaller companies, talk with the factory. Most

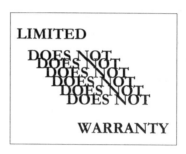

Study the fine print.

have a toll-free number. Have them mail you details. Don't cross off small manufacturers because they have a hundred or less dealerships. These are often the best RVs for the money. Having warranty details in your hand before buy-day is only common sense.

Now that I'm ready to buy, what information do I need to take with me to the dealership?

Since the final step in the buying decision has to do with budget and price, the time has come to have your facts and figures on paper. You should have copies of the MSRP sheets if buying new; and if buying used, you should know the wholesale and retail values. If you have a trade, you'll also want to know its wholesale and retail values.

If you have a worksheet that lists special equipment and services, you'll need it close at hand. Review it at home and be sure it's all clear in your mind. Good salespeople have a great skill for confusing an anxious buyer. As I mentioned before, getting down to within 2% of the very bottom goes beyond skirmishing — it's warfare.

Don't leave home without a brochure that includes the exact unit for which you'll be negotiating and two of the competition's brochures. The competition's brochures are shake-up devices. Any figures you have from the competition should be in your billfold so they don't accidentally fall into the sales-person's hands. It's your secret weapon.

Don't forget your trade-in's title or registration. If you have a payoff, get the figure for approximately ten days after you plan on closing the deal. Don't expect the salesperson to get the payoff for you. He can do it, but it adds another unnecessary variable to the negotiations.

If you've had your trade appraised, or if you've had a cash offer, keep those figures hidden but handy. You need to know them, but it might be to your advantage that the salesperson doesn't know them.

As you prepare these papers for buy-day, think of how much 1% of the retail value will save you in the long run. Each $100 saved will represent about $200 in real savings over a 10-year financing span. Money saved now will improve the quality of those great adventures on your horizon.

Since this one will give me more for the trade, I'll take it instead of...

Play it smart!

Is there an easy way to get a close estimate of payments?

For some, it's easy. For others, working with figures is never easy. I think, however, that anyone who is willing to venture onto our massive and busy highway system with an RV will be able to conquer a simple formula.

You'll need to do some checking on your own for the best current interest rates. As you call each financial institution, get the interest rate and the monthly payment for each $100 financed for the financing term. Since most RVs are sold on a 120 month (10-year) term, you should include that term and one longer or shorter term. This monthly payment for each $100 will make it easy for you to double-check with any figure the dealership gives you.

Let's say the amount you are financing is $10,000. If the bank tells you that your monthly payment is $1.50 for each $100 for a specific term, simply take the last two figures off the finance amount and multiply by $1.50. You can see that your payment for that term with a balance of $10,000 would be $150. Put the information with the name of the bank on a small card. You now have a figure that will put you in control of this part of the negotiations — while keeping you in budget.

Don't lose sight
of type and budget.

This RV has a special price because we've made a deal with the manufacturer to buy a large number of units.

Although possible, it's rarely the case. When Smoothy said this, one manufacturer had discounted a small number of discontinued models. Smoothy exaggerated the purchase in advertising and to prospects.

This tactic must work because Smoothy uses it time and again.

Chapter 23

Rule 9:

*Be prepared to
walk away.*

uy-day has arrived. You've cased the business several
times and are now ready for action. You have your
arsenal of weapons and have girded yourself with the
best armor you can accumulate. You are ready.

Even as you enter the dealership, you must have a
willingness to walk away if anything doesn't feel right. You
know that you have an easy way to escape — just get on your
feet and make them move.

If you find you need thinking space during the negotiations,
take it. If you need a cup of coffee to slow the pace, go to the
local restaurant. If your stomach doesn't feel right, don't take
antacid — take a hike.

You must realize that even if you decide to walk away, a
good salesperson will have techniques designed to stop you.
Some salespeople will stop you before you hit the door. One
of our car salesman students has a successful technique of
stopping a walkaway prospect in mid-stride with a big, "Say!"
It is then back to the table to start over. A true Smoothy loves
the challenge of bringing you back. He's an expert. You're the
novice.

You, however, will be trained to handle the situation. You'll simply turn and say, "We'll see," then leave. The salesperson has your phone number and you have notes. It'll be a draw for now.

If you really want a particular RV and need it now, don't allow the salesperson to know it. Make him or her sweat. Sit in your vehicle a few minutes. It's a poker game. It's now your skill against the skill of the house. If you decide to go back to the desk, do not start over. Continue from where you left off with a review of the facts and figures.

Walking away can save you money. How far you walk depends on your urgency for that particular RV. If the salesperson knows of your urgency, the road will be bumpy. Although there are always too many variables for absolutes, the best way to walk is to go all the way. There's always tomorrow.

Isn't the 5-year plan difficult to keep in focus during the pressure of negotiating?

Anxiety at the closing desk is normal. If you are anxious because you are making an important decision, that's good. If you are simply anxious to get into your new RV, that's bad. Impatience is what the salesperson will look for as a sign of weakness. If your salesperson is a Smoothy, any impatience could cost you between 2% and 5% of the retail value. On buy-day you need to know where you are now and where you're going.

It's time to breathe deep and go slow. If you are married, your spouse should be with you — and you both should agree on all fundamentals before buy-day. If there is any serious disagreement at the dealership, it's best to go home and start over. If the salesperson sees contention, he knows he must overcome the objection and lock it up solid. He knows that every skill he has acquired in sales has to be put into motion.

His thoughts will be running one-way: *"This is the day to close this deal."*

If there are any questions between you and your spouse about your choices, take a last look at your 5-year plan. Ask yourself the following questions: Does the type fit? Does the size fit? Does the brand fit? Does the floor plan fit? Does the final price and payment fit? If you both agree with affirmative answers, then you are ready for buy-day. Let's do it!

How do I know when I'm being ripped off?

If you are entering a dealership with each of the previous 8 rules in place, you'll be safe within 5% of the best deal you can get. On buy-day, you'll be working on that 5%. How much of that 5% you can keep in your savings account will depend on your tenacity to protect every dollar you've accumulated through hard work. To be sure you know where you are, let's look at some percentages and figures.

The gross profit built into most MSRP sheets is between 28% and 32%. There's no way you're going to know the exact gross profit unless you see an invoice and know if there's a volume-bonus in the system. Because of the high cost of keeping an RV on the sales lot, most dealers want to hold a minimum of 15% gross profit. Some will quickly drop to a 12% profit. At the other extreme, I know a few dealers who will accept 8-10% gross profit. Always keep in mind that these profit figures are based on a genuine MSRP retail price. The dealer's personal pricing structure doesn't count.

Because very high percentages of RV buyers allow dealers to get a 20% gross profit, you will help balance the system by working hard to get the dealer to accept a 10% or less gross profit on your deal. Your goal on buy-day is to save dollars, so let's start off by expecting to pay a maximum of 80% of MSRP.

Your worksheet should go this way:

Full Retail:

MSRP	$25,000*
Add-on equipment and services	3,000
Total retail	28,000

Plus:

Freight or Transportation	400
Sales tax (5%)	1,400
License	100
Total price	**$29,900**

You pay:

80% of total retail	22,400
Plus freight	400
Plus tax and license	1,500
plus payoff	1,000
less trade at ACV**	-5,500
Balance due	**$19,800**

*Always work from the MSRP to avoid confusion.
** Actual Cash Value.

I can't afford to give you more than a 12% discount.

If you don't have a trade-in, it's really quite easy now that you have an idea of what discount you'll be working with from the figures in your folder. In the example given, you know you're somewhere near the bottom. The dealer would now have a gross profit between $2,000 and $3,000 (or between 10% and 12%) without add-on equipment. How much he wants to hold depends on his business philosophy and how badly he wants to get rid of a stocked item. How much profit is built into the add-on equipment and services? It's probably somewhere between $1000 and $1500.

Forget MSRP. I'll give you 10% off the special price if you buy today.

If you have a trade, you should be looking at the ACV figure while the dealer is looking at the amount of profit he'll make when he retails the RV. If the deal is close, you'll never know whether he actually considers the trade a plus or minus to the deal. It's in his mind. That's why you work with at least two dealers. They never think the same when it comes to ACV. They treat a trade as a cash outlay, so you need to think of it as a cash value or simply how much cash you can readily get for it on the open market. If you've done your homework, you know this figure. In the example, this is the $5,500 deducted after you subtract the cash discount from the retail price of $28,000.

Now that you have an idea of how to deal with the figures, you know you can have these figures ready on a worksheet of your own in your folder. Make the worksheet so that you understand it. If any serious questions surface during the negotiations, walk! There's always another day.

How do I handle the close?

The close is always pressure. The amount of pressure will depend on how well you've done your homework. A good salesperson will try to get you off your figures and into his.

Keep in mind that you will be fighting to save money and the salesperson will be fighting to keep as much of a commission as he can. If he's any good, he'll manipulate you somehow. You should be ready to put on the brakes or rev the engines — whatever the situation calls for. Remember, you're supposed to be in control.

Try to put the salesperson out of his comfort zone by negotiating in the RV. By taking the salesperson away from his desk, the telephone, and the sales manager, you will be taking some of his control. However, if you get him to accept your offer, don't sign papers in the RV. The final acceptance of both parties must be done where you won't be distracted from studying the "fine print."

Because selling is with us every day,
it's hard to turn and walk away.

If you have a sharp salesperson, watch for the following techniques:

1) use of words,
2) pleasant conversation,
3) turning the paperwork (contract) to you,
4) passing of the pen,
5) pleading look,
6) a touch of impatience,
7) "Time is now" attitude,
8) a resell of the features,
9) a resell on the price, and
10) putting pressure on the urgency factor. If the salesperson's adrenaline is flowing, he's in the best of form. This is the time to watch out.

You are now an expert buyer. Your adrenaline is flowing because you're ready for great adventures. You're thinking how every dollar saved here will take you that extra mile. You're not going to let any salesperson turn you into a robot. Victory is within your reach. Don't blow it!

*Congratulations on your new trailer!
To show our appreciation for the business,
the sales manager has approved giving you a
complete pre-delivery inspection for $75
instead of the regular price of $250.*

This one worked like a charm! I'd never heard it before and I'm not sure that Smoothy had ever tried it before. But since he picked up another $20 commission quick-like, I'm sure he'll try it again.

Of course, not everyone knows that most RV manufacturers pay for pre-delivery inspection. But now you do!

Chapter 24

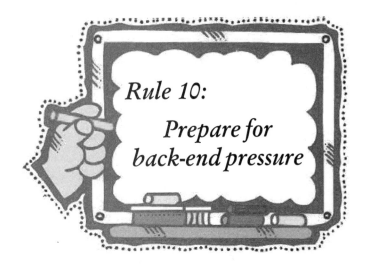

Rule 10:

*Prepare for
back-end pressure*

B ack-end sales should not be an issue with most of you because few of you want these services or products. Big profits are made at RV dealerships from back-end sales. It's called back-end because they get the buyer in the back-end after the close — which the buyer thinks is the end. Back-end sales come from financing, insurance, extended warranties, and interior and exterior protection packages. Profits are so high in percentages that they are hard to compute. Profits from interest above the dealer buy-rate are often astronomical. Extended warranties are usually in the 50% gross profit area or higher. The list goes on, and the profits stay high.

The pressure exerted by dealer management for back-end sales is always high. The average back-end expert (called the finance manager, F & I officer, or business manager) earns between $50,000 and $100,000 a year. They are the Smoothies of Smoothies. Compared to the average salesperson, BEE (back-end expert) is a real stinger.

You will never prepare enough for BEE if you've selected a high pressure dealership for buy-day. You can, however, make it a learning experience and walk away without it costing you. You can simply say "No!" to everything. You've come a long way in learning to save thousands of dollars, so don't blow it now by letting your guard down.

In smaller neighborhood dealerships, the back-end services are often sold by the salesperson. In this scenario, it's easy to handle. If he finds you are reluctant, the salesperson won't jeopardize the sale by putting on too much pressure. Because the commissions are good, however, expect almost anything. All you need to say is "No!" and the subject should be dropped.

We said "NO!" and he wasn't even upset!

If you think you might consider an extended warranty, payment insurance, or any RV interior or exterior coating protection, you should have inquired as to the cost and benefits during your research. If you wait until buy-day, you'll find the temptation as high as your urgency to hit the road. Do it before buy-day.

Are you saying that dealers make money on financing?

You bet your pretty monthly payments they do! Every RV dealer gets buy-rates from financial institutions. This buy-rate can be near prime. Any difference between the buy-rate and the interest rate charged on the contract will find itself in a trust account designated for the dealership. The details may be different with each financial institution, but the purpose of this system is to encourage dealers to work hard to get financing away from your own sources. Consider how much a dealer would make if the interest rate charged to you is 10% and the dealer's buy rate is 8%. That 2% interest will be going to the dealer every month. At that percentage you can simply figure about 20% of the interest you pay will be going to the dealer. Do you want the dealer to get thousands of your hard-earned dollars for a few minutes of paperwork that should have been included in the deal? Of course not!

All this shows the importance of active research to get a good interest rate. Work the phone. Call all local banks. Call your credit union. Look in the paper for specials on interest rates. If you do this, you'll be prepared to negotiate when you're ushered into BEE's office. Work him to the lowest rate before you give him yours. BEE makes his living from getting a "Yes" from you. Be ready to fight BEE. If his stinger gets in, it's going to stay for years.

Keep in mind that these rules apply to autos and trucks. After all, that's where the RV industry learned to wheel and deal.

Be sure you say it this way, "I've a real deal for you today!"

How do I know if I need payment protection insurance?

Usually payment insurance is too expensive for most of us. It is possible for older people to get good deals because there is no health check. If, for example, you are approaching 60, have a heart problem, are spending most of your money reserves on an RV, and your surviving spouse would have a hard time making the RV payments, you may want to consider a simple program. Unless you feel the odds are against your living through the financing term, go strictly for decreasing term. Consider this only if your debt-to-income ratio is high and life expectancy is low. To be sure, compare with regular insurance companies.

Oh yes! I remember the advice I gave to my wonderful children.

Sweet BEE

If you get confused about the cost, ask for accurate payment figures before the insurance is added and again after it's added. Be sure BEE gives you these figures in writing. Multiply the difference times the number of payments for the real cost. Other figures don't really count.

Know these things: BEE knows how to push. BEE knows how to scare. BEE works on anxiety and conscience. BEE comes across as a nice person. Often BEE will be a mother or grandfather type. BEE is always concerned for you. BEE gets your shields down. BEE always earns lots of money. BEE often functions on guile. BEE is always a Smoothy!

They want **what** figures?

Ask before you go in!

What about extended warranties?

Generally, extended warranties are not a good buy. Like payment protection, however, there is a scenario where an extended warranty may be worth considering. If you purchase an almost new motor home which has had questionable care, if you are taking long voyages away from home, if you have no road-smarts, if your travel budget has been shot by the purchase, and if it makes you feel better even with the larger payment, an extended warranty might be worth considering. Otherwise, do not consider it a smart buy.

If you decide to consider an extended warranty, investigate the underwriter. Be absolutely clear what the policy does not cover. BEE is going to try very hard to sell you on this product. The commissions are big. A word of extreme caution: Most RV and auto buyers go in determined not to buy an extended warranty — but BEE makes the sting. Most buyers get it in the end.

What are the real costs of these 'back-end' services?

If you're having the purchase financed, double the quoted cost and you'll be pretty close to the real cost. If you're a cash buyer, figure how much you'd gain in interest over the normal financing term and add it to the quoted cost.

BEE will not want to do it, but get exact payments on the RV purchase before going into the "business office." As BEE finishes with each step, get new monthly payment figures in writing. Multiply the difference times the term. You'll soon see the real costs. And please, just because BEE seems to be a busy BEE, don't let him or her rush you. BEE is very astute. BEE is quick. Unlike RV salespeople, almost every BEE you meet will be a professional. There are few sloppy BEE's in the world. Beat BEE by practicing to say,

NO!

How do I know that I've gotten the best deal possible?

You don't. The important thing is that you've done the best you could— and better than 90% of RV buyers worldwide.

When you leave the dealership, it's time to celebrate the adventure of buying an RV without getting ripped off. It's time to celebrate for the adventures that are just around the corner and over the next hill. It's time to move out — to hit the road.

In closing . . .

I must emphasize that the attitude and performance of RV salespeople are the symptoms, not the cause, of a haphazard and often destructive demeanor toward the RV consumer. RV manufacturers are the cause of the condition. Their overall performance has been mediocre at best. At worst, manufacturers have performed with greed and profit as their only props, while social conscience lay covered with dust just off stage. This attitude is infectious to those who sit in the audience.

RV manufacturers have an audience made up of retailers and their employees. This audience rarely throws tomatoes because its bread and butter comes from the manufacturers. Retailers know that their influence is minimal. The power is in the hands of the builders. Dealers sell what they get. They tell me they do what they must do to survive.

Once again I would like to quote from excerpts of my articles in *the RV Lookout,* the first newsletter published by RV Consumer Group:

"My experiences with RV manufacturers have been so depressing that it's difficult for me to think positively. I've seen so many people cheated out of a lifetime of accumulated assets that "shocking" becomes an inadequate word. When you find unsophisticated and uncaring RV manufacturers making millions by marketing products with little substance, you must wonder about it all. I am probably not unlike the reporter who visits a starving nation and finds too few words to express the emotion that overshadows the task. I am not a radical — my Scottish blood keeps me from that extreme. I am not hard — my French blood keeps me tingling. I am just an RVer who loves the lifestyle.

"The RV industry is in its infancy. It is now where the auto industry was in the early '30s — the decade of GM's beginning and Ford's Model A. No sense of social conscience has yet evolved from the hundreds of companies that are vying for market share in this very competitive atmosphere. It's like babes in the woods — babes of the Paul Bunyan size, large enough to destroy the forest. It's a time comparable to the gold rush days, with an obvious difference — few of the participants are drowning, freezing to death, or dying from shoot-outs. Industry fatalities are low because the lack of available consumer information keeps profits high for the bad as well as for the good. This is status quo protected. It shouldn't be this way. Good RV manufacturers should be bound by a sense of social conscience and mutual survival.

"The American consumer is vengeful, however. We've proved time and again that there's a limit to our patience. Although we've given the RV industry a bonanza of riches, they've thrown toys at our feet. We want more than toys. We want substance. We want RVs that will last. We want good products and fair dealings. We want the American RV industry to do for RVers what the Japanese have done for the auto consumer. As RV consumers, we want fair treatment from those with whom we spend our savings. It's time for all of us to open our eyes to see beyond the next hill."

You can tell from your voyage through this book that I do not excuse RV dealers and salespeople for having an indifferent or belligerent attitude toward the RV consumer. I have shown you that you are vulnerable to their excesses of greed and profit. RV dealers know that everything I tell you is true, although most will quickly declare, "Not me!"

You, as the consumer, have the power to put it right. You, as the consumer, can put unscrupulous RV dealers out of business in a very short time. You can do this by sticking to the ten rules in this book.

If you buy an RV with the determination to make it a good investment, you'll choose correctly. You'll begin with type and end with price. You won't let anyone turn this around. You'll stay on course and keep that $6,000 to improve your adventures. You'll learn as you prepare questions to ask salespeople. You'll enjoy your new-found ability to inquire like an expert. You won't be a real expert, of course, but you'll feel like one because you'll know more than most of the so-called experts you'll meet on your rounds.

As you leave the many dealerships you visit to get you started, you'll find yourself often vowing never to return. You'll begin to shake your head as you recognize line after line of bull and more bull. When you eliminate half the dealerships you visit, you'll feel good about what you've learned and where you're going.

You won't get caught up in the trust game. You've learned enough to tread carefully when RV salespeople start spouting off about specials, sales, and discounts. You'll know what to expect when they start to put on the pressure. You'll have your escape plans tied to your feet — and you'll use them often.

You won't put up with a tour when a presentation is needed. You'll know how to ask. You'll know what to expect. If it doesn't go the way it should, you'll know how to lead. One way or another, you'll learn about the product.

By now you know enough to keep quality in focus. You'll associate brand with quality and have an idea which manufacturers are building acceptable RVs. You won't be overwhelmed by the many claims because you won't let glitter cloud your eyesight.

You know that eventually you'll get down to choosing two dealerships for buy-day. When you get down to this number, you'll have the tools to work one against the other and not feel bad about doing it. You'll expect to save thousands of dollars, and you'll know that it's your right to fight for the best deal you can get.

Your basic tools will be paper, pen, and *The RV Ratings Guide* CD. You'll combine these tools with brochures to build an arsenal that will take you to victory. You'll prepare a step at a time and then you'll give it your all. You'll know you're going to win.

When buy-day arrives, you'll be prepared to walk away if things aren't as they should be. You'll know that there's always tomorrow. You'll take the time to review your preparation and check your 5-year plan. You won't let anyone rush you into a deal that's not to your advantage.

You will, of course, be prepared for back-end pressure. By now you have a good picture of what to expect beyond the RV purchase. You'll know how to say "No!" and you'll remember how to use your feet. You won't let BEE rub his hands in glee after you leave the dealership.

There is more to learn than what is in this book, but what you have learned is a good beginning. If you follow the ten basic rules, you will save thousands of dollars and have a good chance of buying an RV that will fit into your 5-year plan. No system is guaranteed to keep Smoothy at bay — but without a system, Smoothy will most assuredly keep getting richer and you'll keep getting poorer.

If you need help, remember that all of us at RV Consumer Group are here to help. You need not do it alone.

Happy trekking!

JD

Sharing a bit about the author —

JD being interviewed for a
television news consumer segment. (1999)

JD in one of his first appraisal workshops offered
to RV Consumer Group members. (circa 1992)

Connie and JD Gallant
(circa...a while ago)

RVCG's founding member and Connie's mother, the
late Maria Bernardo, shown here with JD and Connie's
home on wheels (converted school bus) and pleasure
craft. (circa 1986)

JD and Connie's first fulltiming rig — the trailer served as Connie's photo darkroom. (circa 1977)

The buying terms shown in this section
are excerpted from *The Language of RVing*,
a full glossary of words and terms included in
RV Consumer Group's *RV Ratings Guide CD*.

Buying Terms

from
The Language of RVing

Glossary

actual cash value:

To a dealership, the real value of any RV is its actual cash value (ACV). The salesperson may talk wholesale or retail value, but in the back of his or her mind there's a figure of the real worth that must be used to calculate trade. Normally, ACV is the book wholesale value plus or minus condition, options, size, floor plan, interior colors, and other factors that influence salability.

For example, if a 30-foot 1985 motor home with twin beds, orange interior, and a small dent on the side is being considered as a trade-in, the wholesale value might be $10,000, but because of the condition and the unpopularity of the length, floor plan, and color, the salesperson might give it an ACV of $8,600. The salesperson will also consider the length of time the RV might sit on the lot. Of course, if the RV is in exceptional condition, the positives could give the unit an ACV above the book wholesale figure. The ACV will be the same amount the dealership would pay in cash.

Having been both an RV buyer and RV salesperson, I know how hard it is to find out if a trade-in allowance is fair. The easiest way to do this is 1) get a quote from three RV dealers who are receptive toward buying your RV outright, and 2) get wholesale figures from at least two RV appraisal books. Average the two highest bids and the two appraisal book figures and you will have a fair ACV value. Add the normal no-trade discount of the RV you are buying and you'll have a good basis for a trade-in allowance.

Most of us think our RVs are worth more than they actually are, but I've also found too many who have practically given their RVs away. Knowing the real value of your RV will help make you a happy camper.

back-end:

The "back-end" is a term used to refer to the selling of services after the sale of the vehicle. Back-end selling is usually conducted by a F&I (finance and insurance) officer, business manager, or finance manager. In small dealerships, the salesperson or sales manager may sell back-end services.

Back-end gross profits to the dealership usually equal or exceed the gross profit on the vehicle sale. These services include financing, payment protection, life insurance, extended service coverage, and various vehicle coatings. A buyer should be aware that he or she will be exposed to high-pressure selling of these services.

blue book: See *Kelley Blue Book.*

brand name:

Whenever you go into an electronics store you probably notice that big promotions begin with the name. The name is almost everything in electronics equipment. This emphasis on brand name is the result of good promotions and public demand for good electronics products. We all know there are some names in stereos, televisions, and video recorders that are considered safe buys. Because of this, those of us who are habitual shoppers choose the brand name and then shop for a price.

In the RV industry, name identification has a long way to go. It is unfortunate that three out of every four RV shoppers can't connect the brand name with an RV manufacturer. The proliferation of new brand names from major manufacturers who want to capture a larger share of the market keeps complicating the problem. Still another reason for the problem has been the ease of getting into the RV manufacturing business. Small companies can emerge, build a good-looking product, and the uninformed RV public will gobble it up. The process may be healthy for the free enterprise system, but it can be very costly to the RV consumer.

The major motor home manufacturers — *Fleetwood, Winnebago, Holiday Rambler, National, Rexhall, Tiffen, Country Coach, Monaco, Coachmen,* and others — are eager to capture you as a customer. Once you know the reputation of the manufacturer of any brand, you will be able to make better choices. Like most consumer products, RVs can be rated. Due to the lack of regulation, the consistency of the RV industry to produce a good product is much worse than quality consistency in the automobile industry. For this reason you must be more diligent in your consideration of brand name.

Brand names are so important to your investment factor that you should never invest in an RV without investigating the manufacturer. The philosophy of the parent corporation in regard to providing a good product will show up with a minimum of research. A good manufacturer will build a good product at a good value. Quality of workmanship will never be cut by good RV manufacturers because they have reputations to protect. Good manufacturers hire good workers at all their plants and back their products with good warranties. Good RV manufacturers will produce RVs that will protect your investment.

As you begin your search for an RV, look at the brand name before you look at anything else. Look the salesperson straight in the eye as you ask about the manufacturer. Watch for answers without hesitation. As you go about the unit, compare quality in workmanship and materials with the statements the salesperson makes about the manufacturer. If you begin to think this way, you might consider buying only from established manufacturers who have been around long enough to have a history. When you realize that all brands are not created equal, you'll have learned that RV value begins with the name.

buy-rate:

RV dealers can make money during buyer financing by getting a share of the interest money. They do this by getting a buy-rate from financial institutions, then adding a profit to that rate. Some dealers will hold that profit to a fraction of a percentage point to cover costs of the financing office, but some get greedy and tack on as many full percentage points as the unwary buyer will tolerate.

buyer's agreement:

When you approve the basic price of an RV with options, sales tax, license, and trade-in value subject to other terms and conditions, you have concluded a buyer's agreement. When you tell the salesperson that you want the RV to be taken off the market and be prepared to your specifications, the buyer's agreement becomes a buyer's order. The buyer's order is a legal and binding contract between you and the dealership. The terms written across the face of the buyer's agreement must be explicit enough to allow you an opportunity to cancel the order if something goes awry.

cash conversion:

The term "cash conversion" describes the salesperson's approach to persuade the cash buyer that it is better to finance than to pay cash. The advantages stressed will be that the buyer will be able to get cheap payment protection, will have cash available for other needs, may be able to get income tax credits for interest paid, and might be able to invest cash in programs that will allow for more income through interest or dividends than expenses in interest paid on the loan. The primary purpose of the cash conversion is to open more doors for insurance and other back-end services. Each buyer should study this proposal with the same care used for the purchase price of the RV. If you are resigned to writing a check for your RV, I recommend that you hold the course when approached with the cash conversion angle.

consignment:

RVers are very prone to changing their minds and wanting a different RV type, floor plan, size, or brand. It doesn't mean that RVers are fickle (although I think that most of us are), but RVers often outgrow the unit they thought would last them for 10 to 20 years after only 3 or 4 years. Because getting another RV isn't as simple as it may seem at first, you might want to consign your old RV to an RV dealer to get cash instead of trading it in on a new unit. If this choice is made, there are two basic consignment programs that you will need to understand.

The first and most common consignment program is one where the dealer keeps a specific percentage of the selling price. This usually varies between 10 and 15 percent to cover advertising costs, space, and delivery preparations. If you go for the percentage basis, you will need to know the selling price and immediately deduct the percentage and any payoff to the bank to find out what you'll realize in your pocket.

The other way to enter the consignment program is to demand a specific amount for the unit and let the dealership keep what it can get over that amount. This works well with a dealership that takes in many trades because trading requires high figures at both ends of the deal. I personally like this program because it's always difficult to explain the real value of a trade-in to the RV owner who is scrutinizing the whole deal to be sure he gets his share.

Consigning has some good advantages that should be considered unless you are a natural salesperson and have a readily salable unit.

deposit:

When you have agreed to specific terms of purchase on an RV that you want, you should put a deposit of good faith on the order. The deposit should be given with the condition that specific terms — such as the time required to arrange financing — are written on the order. The deposit usually takes the unit off the market for a specific number of days, but deposits by themselves should not authorize a get-ready order.

down payment:

The down payment is a percentage of the total amount required by the loaning institution. If the terms are cash, the down payment may be any amount required by the dealership to conclude the terms of purchase and begin the order or get-ready process. If a deposit has been made, this amount will become part of the down payment.

extended service contract:

When you buy a new or a pre-owned RV, the dealership may offer you an extended service contract. (Because salespeople rarely call anything a contract, it might be called an extended service agreement.) For a new RV, the service contract begins at the end of the manufacturer's warranty term. Price of an extended service contract can vary from about $1500 to $5,000 or more for a motor home. Motor homes usually have mileage limitations between 60,000 and 100,000 miles.

Major considerations when buying an extended service contract should be the policy underwriters and the deductible. If the underwriter is known to be financially stable and the deductible is reasonable for the annual fee, ponder it as you would the RV price and the terms for financing. If you plan on living in the unit, it is especially important that you consider it seriously since fulltiming maintenance costs can be extensive. In some cases, it might be a good idea to give up an accessory for the service contract.

fair-market value:

Fair-market value is a figure used by the insurance industry and the IRS to compute a realistic value on the item. For example, if you wrecked your RV and didn't want it repaired, you would try to convince the insurance company of the fair-market value so they would cash you out with enough to buy a comparable unit. The IRS might try to determine fair-market value for an item donated to a charitable organization.

The fair-market value of an RV is the amount you should be able to realize after exerting reasonable effort and advertising. When using a value appraisal book, fair-market value could be anywhere between wholesale and retail.

guarantee:

When you assure someone that nothing will go wrong and back up that assurance with a bond for damages resulting from the malfunction, you have created a guarantee. A guarantee usually implies a specific remuneration whereas a warranty is less specific in its terms.

high book:

High book is a term used by auto and RV dealers. It means the same as retail price.

hold:

Salespeople will generally accept a certain amount of money to hold or keep a unit reserved for the customer for a specific period. When the terms of the purchase are established, a customer may leave a check or cash to allow enough time to arrange for financing or other requirements. A hold should be refundable and should be so written on the buyer's agreement.

interest rate:

Because RVs, unlike homes and autos, are considered luxury items, some banks consider the risks of repossession higher and impose higher interest rates for financing these purchases. If you take the time to study the financing figures, you'll find that half a percent can make a big difference in the monthly payment — and thus the overall cost of the RV. It's easy to get on the phone and call the various banks and RV dealerships to determine the best rate available.

investment factor:

If you want to figure on getting a monetary return in addition to pleasure from your RV, you will need to determine an investment factor based on the monetary cost of owning an RV. The investment factor can thus be considered the percentage of return you will get for your original investment. Try to think of investment factor as the amount you'll get in cash value when you sell or trade your RV in relation to the amount you spent. If your investment factor is 50 percent after owning an RV for 10 years, you are about average — but probably could have done much better. If your return is 70 percent of the original cost, you have done very well.

Figuring an investment factor is one way of determining how your new RV will hold its value. We all know that as soon as you leave the dealership, the value of your new unit will drop to or below the wholesale price. This means that you'll probably need to keep the RV from 5 to 10 years at an average inflation rate of about 6 percent to get 60 or 70 percent of your original outlay returned.

Because the investment factor is based upon salability at some time in the future, the price you pay and the quality of the RV will be the two most important factors. By buying a lower-priced unit that has a good reputation for holding together, you can increase the investment factor. On the other hand, if you invest in a unit that will fall apart, your investment factor will be low. Of course, buying the unit below the manufacturer's suggested retail price will always improve the investment factor.

Size also hurts the investment factor. Some of the long trailers will suffer major depreciation no matter how long they are kept. The investment factor will change as the demand for length, floor plan, and interior design changes. Anyone looking seriously toward a high investment factor will study RV trends as an investor in the stock market would study trends in the national economy.

Good maintenance is always a requirement for keeping a high resale value. Because most of us put off doing maintenance, we should look at RV characteristics that minimize maintenance. Better appliances, superb workmanship, quality materials, and good design all help to keep an RV in good condition for 20 years or longer.

Although size, colors, floor plan, design, and price affect the investment factor, nothing affects it like the name. A brand that is reasonably priced and has a reputation for holding together will always have the highest return on the original cost.

I found out that where you live can also influence the investment factor. Because acid rain contains sulfur, sulfur dioxide, and nitric oxide, it is important that you flush and wash your RV as often as possible. These chemicals can cause damage to the RV's surface. An etching and a dulling of the surface is bound to happen if you get into an area where acid rain is common; but it can be minimized with a mild soap washing. Special cleansers are required if etching does occur. Paying attention to the outside of the RV will give you a higher investment factor and not cost you the $1,000 in depreciation that it cost me.

Budgets limit us to an amount we can spend. Budgets mean that we have to be careful that we don't overspend. When RV shopping, we often find that we can put off getting many of the options until a later date. By not buying options with the RV, you can take a step upward in quality to increase the investment factor. Awning, TV antenna, air conditioning, and microwave are important only if you need them and can afford them. First consider that the flexibility allowed by a good investment might be what you'll need down the road.

invoice:

When you talk about invoice while dealing for an RV, you'll actually be referring to dealer cost. A good dealership will not show you the invoice under any conditions, because they know that the practice could open up price wars and questionable promotion tactics that have long been associated with the auto industry. The auto and the RV industries are distinctly different in the way they must serve the needs of the public, and I hope it will stay that way. If the RV dealer, however, says that he'll give you dealer invoice plus some other figure, you should be shown the invoice from the RV manufacturer then add the figure that was negotiated. A price negotiated from invoice doesn't mean much if you don't see the invoice once earnest money is presented and all other terms are met.

Kelley Blue Book:

The *Kelley Blue Book* (copyrighted by *Kelley Blue Book* Co., Irvine, California 92718) is distributed to automotive and RV dealerships to estimate the value of used vehicles. The *Kelley Blue Book* lists all RVs in alphabetical order and gives the models, weight, manufacturer's suggested retail price when new, the current average wholesale value, and the current average retail value. The values are for the base units and do not include add-on options. There is a list of options with values in the front of the book. The book must be current and should be considered only as an estimate of value since condition is a big factor in the actual cash value. Because banks often use appraisal books as a guide for lending money, the wholesale value is often called loan value.

lemon laws:

Almost every state has a lemon law to protect new motor vehicle buyers, and a few states have laws that protect used motor vehicle buyers. This protection varies greatly from state to state. It generally protects the consumer when a vehicle fails sufficiently to warrant repeated returns to the dealership with subsequent loss of the use of the vehicle. To win a lemon law case, it is imperative that the vehicle owner keep accurate records to substantiate losses in time and money due to the failure. If there is any question about your vehicle being eligible for lemon law protection, call your state attorney general.

license estimate:

When the amount of the license is included in the buyer's agreement, it is usually an estimated figure. Although most salespeople know the license costs within 20 percent, some states have formulas so complex that it might require a call to the licensing department to get the exact license figure. If the figure is approximate, the salesperson should write 'license estimate' on the buyer's agreement to let you know that you will either get a refund or need to pay more.

limited warranty:

All warranties are somewhat limited, but good manufacturers extend warranty coverage over one year to *all* components of the RV. What this means to you is that the local dealership will assist you in handling claims against any component that fails during the RV's warranty term. Limited warranties may have exclusions for transfer of ownership, use as a residence, travel out of the country, and components not built by the RV manufacturer. If the brochure even mentions 'limited' when it explains its warranty coverage, send for a copy of warranty terms from the manufacturer.

low book:

The wholesale price of a vehicle in a value appraisal book is also known as low book.

manufacturer's suggested retail price:

At the bottom of the pricing structure we have invoice, and at the top we have manufacturer's suggested retail price (MSRP). The invoice is the wholesale price and the MSRP is the retail price. The retail price can be any figure the dealer wants it to be. The MSRP can be ignored by the dealer who can ask any amount he wants for the unit. Here lies the danger: Unless you know the MSRP you can't know what the builder thinks the RV is worth. Unless you know the MSRP, you must rely upon your experiences and the word of the salesperson to determine the value of any RV. Unless you know the MSRP, you won't have a basis by which to compare values with other RVs. Very simply, you must know the MSRP to begin establishing a value for the unit.

An MSRP sheet should be sent with each RV from the plant where it was built. The MSRP sheet will tell you:

1) the model,
2) the serial number,
3) where it was built,
4) all the items normally included in the building of that model,
5) optional items included in the RV,
6) the basic retail price of the unit,
7) the retail price of the options, and
8) the total manufacturer's suggested retail price.

Sometimes freight and dealer preparation costs will be included in the MSRP total figure. Some manufacturers send a color-banded MSRP sheet with each new unit. This computer printout will reflect what the manufacturer thinks is a fair retail value for that particular unit based upon the building cost. As you compare one RV with another, MSRP sheets will give you a good beginning for establishing values of the various brands. As you compare manufacturers, however, keep in mind that the MSRP *does not guarantee value.*

All manufacturers should furnish MSRP sheets with each new RV. A color-banded MSRP sheet will keep those retail figures honest. It will let you, the consumer, make choices based on those figures. All RV buyers should ask to see the manufacturer's suggested retail price sheet. The original MSRP sheets should be kept in a book in the dealership office while *unaltered* copies are placed in the RV. These color-banded MSRP sheets should be readily shown to you upon request. The manufacturer allows the dealer a very generous profit. The dealer can hold that profit or drop it — that will be his choice. For you to make an intelligent choice, you need to know the MSRP. Remember, it's *your* savings that are being spent.

N.A.D.A. Appraisal Guide:

The *N.A.D.A. Appraisal Guide* is an estimating guide for values on used automobiles and RVs. Published periodically by the *National Automobile Dealer's Association.*

optional equipment:

On some RVs the optional equipment list is quite long. The difference between standard equipment, standard options, and optional equipment is often confusing to new RVers. Standard equipment is automatically included in the construction of the RV and usually cannot be deleted. Standard-run options are put on stock RVs for sale to dealers, and these options will usually show on the MSRP sheet to the right of the standard equipment. Standard-run options can be deleted by special order. With some manufacturers, special options are available by special order during the time of building. Of course, many options are available at the dealership that may not be available from the manufacturer. Although options at the dealership may not be as negotiable as the completed unit, a buyer should be aware that dealer-installed options can become part of the negotiated package.

out-the-door:

If a salesperson tells you that you can have the unit for a certain out-the-door price, they are usually referring to the price of the unit with appropriate sales tax and license. Never assume, however, that an out-the-door figure means anything that is not written on the buyer's order.

When you sit down with the RV salesperson, be friendly. If you're going to get the deal you want, you're going to get it because of firmness — not from being cantankerous. If you become an adversary and the salesperson finds out that you don't know what you think you know, the facts will be twisted to his or her advantage. Be friendly, be firm, be fair, and be quick to leave if you don't think you're being treated right. Remember, you can't go wheeling until you've done your dealing.

payment protection:

An item that every RV buyer should consider is payment protection due to death or disability. This is an insurance program that is especially valuable to persons getting close to retirement age. Because payment protection does not usually take the age of the applicant into consideration (to the maximum limit) for rate setting, it can be very affordable insurance for those over 50.

When you consider life payment protection, you should realize that there are two types: gross and net. With gross coverage you build a sort of equity into the policy — but only during the policy term. Net is simply decreasing term insurance, giving you coverage for the payment only. It is obviously cheaper and is adequate for most people. Disability coverage should be looked at by those still in the work force with heavy financial obligations. What I am stressing here is that you investigate payment protection as part of the financing program. Don't automatically rule it out!

payment term:

Too many people look only at the payment when they're considering an RV purchase. If you aren't careful about the term, you might find out that the RV depreciates much faster than the loan balance disappears. The term should be based upon the practical life of the unit being purchased. If you are buying a brand that has a questionable reputation, you should probably consider a 24-to-60 month term. On a new unit from a quality manufacturer, a 10-year term is not unreasonable if you plan on keeping it for a while. I personally do not advocate financing over 10 years on motor homes. *Quality* fulltiming RVs could be financed to 12 years if necessary.

qualifying:

A salesperson qualifies a prospective buyer to determine capability of buying a product or sincere interest in buying a product. By using good qualifying techniques, a salesperson will quickly determine how much time to spend with the prospect and what manipulative techniques will work best.

We all know that the best qualifying techniques often backfire, but the process is so ingrained in most salespeople that it's as automatic as eating.

A good RV salesperson will discreetly ask a few basic what, when, where, why, and how questions to determine what kind of assistance is needed and then get into a good presentation and allow the customer to make the choices.

secret warranty:

This term is often used to describe notifying vehicle owners of defects found in their RVs (or autos) by public notice. Although not applicable in every case, RV owners should be aware that recall notices are not always mailed. If you hear of a recall through any source, check with the vehicle manufacturer to see if it applies to you.

signature:

If you "okay" or "approve" a buyer's agreement with your name, you have made a legal commitment by affixing your signature. If, however, you have not taken possession of the vehicle, you may only be obligated for costs of preparations you have ordered.

standard equipment:

Every new RV comes with standard equipment. Standard equipment is usually listed in the brochure and on the left side of the MSRP (manufacturer's suggested retail price) sheet. Standard equipment is included in the unit price and usually cannot be deleted. There are, however, optional upgrades that can replace many items on the standard equipment list. A buyer should always check the standard equipment list to find out exactly what is included with the unit. The brand and specifications of standard equipment are important.

subject to...:

    You should never enter into RV buying negotiations without an understanding of how to control the buying terms. Although most RV dealerships are basically honest, the terms written on the buyer's agreement by the salesperson will be considered a contract once the order is signed by the buyer. To avoid unpleasant misunderstandings, simply write any questionable terms after the statement "subject to..." on the face of the buyer's agreement. "Subject to a financing rate of 10 percent," is an example. "Subject to approval of road test by buyers," is a good one for motor home buyers. "Subject to acceptable financing terms," will give you an easy out if you need it. Whatever you do, be sure the 'subject to' statement is clearly written on the buyer's agreement if there is any question about the purchase terms.

trade-in allowance:

    The allowance given for a trade-in will reflect the actual cash value of the RV plus any given cash discount from the retail or asking price of the unit being purchased.

trial close:

    When an RV salesperson starts leading you to the sales office before you indicate a desire to buy, he or she is using a trial close technique. The trial close will be a test of your resistance to his or her methods of selling. Statements like, "Let's see what the payments are on this model," will indicate that you are being tested.

    The best way to avoid getting trial closes will be to leave your emotions at home. Since this is almost impossible to do when buying an RV, at least keep them under control. Try not to give buying signals like, "Wow! This is just perfect for my needs."

    All good salespeople look for buying signals and are ready with a trial close. Control of the buying process is always yours. Don't give it away.

turn:

    "Turn" is a term used at dealerships to indicate the process of bouncing a prospect from salesperson to salesperson to sales manager. The idea is to give other salespeople a chance at closing the prospective buyer. The term comes from the auto industry where turns are common and often mandatory. If you feel yourself being bounced like a yo-yo during the buying process, you'll know that you have been "turned."

upside down:

    Being upside down is the unhappy condition of owing more for a vehicle than it's worth. The causes for being upside down can be paying too much for the vehicle, trying to trade it or sell it too soon after the purchase, or getting involved in a bad financing program. In the RV world, the problem is serious because many RVers want to trade or sell before half the financing term has been reached.

warranty:

A warranty stipulates in writing the terms for covering any malfunction in your RV. Although you will always receive some sort of warranty from a manufacturer, warranties may also be issued by a dealership to cover specific repairs or components for used units. You must be sure that the warranty is explicit. Always ask to see a copy of the terms of the warranty since it is difficult to enforce performance of an implied warranty.

Good RV manufacturers issue a warranty to cover all aspects of their product for a specific length of time. Be sure that the word "limited" is not incorporated into the warranty without your knowing where it is limited. You should study the warranty as you would study the buyer's agreement and financing contract.

wholesale:

Every RV dealership must make a profit on the RVs they sell. To make a profit, they buy or take in trades at a wholesale value and sell them at a retail value. Although the difference between wholesale and retail usually reflects approximately 30% gross profit, daily interest charges on inventory (flooring) and other costs of keeping an RV on the sales lot can easily consume much of this. The wholesale value of a new RV is often called invoice. The wholesale value of a used RV is usually determined by using the *Kelley Blue Book* or the *N.A.D.A. Appraisal Guide*.

Zzzz:

RVers: Don't sleep on the job! Entering the RVing lifestyle is a challenging affair. If you take it as anything else, you are probably going to be disappointed and disillusioned very shortly.

May smart RV consumers and good RV salespeople meet in campgrounds across America.

JD Gallant

Your RV Inspection List

Use this brief list to get you started in the inspection process of a new or used RV. For a more detailed inspection checklist, please check RV Consumer Group's Forms page at rv.org. The chart at the end of this form lists the numerical scoring you can use for each section you inspect.

Year_____ Brand_____ Model_____

Outside: **Notes**

Profile   _____

Skin   _____

Structure   _____

Roof   _____

Chassis   _____

Inside

Galley   _____

Bathroom   _____

Woodwork   _____

Lining   _____

Fixtures   _____

Notes:

_____

_____

_____

_____

_____

_____

_____

_____

_____

_____

_____

_____

_____

_____

Notes:

_____

_____

_____

_____

_____

_____

_____

_____

Scoring

10	—	Excellent
9	—	Very good
8	—	Good
7	—	Good with reservations
6	—	Fair
5	—	Poor
4	—	Not acceptable
3	—	Seriously flawed
2	—	Extremely flawed
1	—	Total disaster

I recommend that you keep a list of routine service checks on your RV — it will make your life easier and your RV's life running smoother.

RV ROUTINE SERVICE CHECKS

ITEM	Monthly	Quarterly	Semi-annual	Annual
Check & adjust tire pressure	X			
Check coolant level	X			
Check engine oil level	X			
Check transmission oil level	X			
Check power steering reservoir		X		
Check windshield fluid level	X			
Check radiator, heater & AC hoses			X	
Check for worn tires	X			
Flush underside of vehicle			X	
Check headlight alignment		X		
Check spare tire air pressure		X		
Treat gaskets with 303			X	
Check battery electrolyte		X		
Check battery terminals		X		
Lubricate door/storage hinges			X	
Check operation of:				
Lamps	X			
Horn	X			
Turn signals	X			
Hazard warning flashers	X			
Windshield wipers	X			

RV Consumer Group

is a nonprofit organization that

Rates RVs

‣ It is primarily operated by a professional staff of employees and volunteers.

‣ It has been conducting RV buying workshops and publishing books for many years.

‣ Ratings are shown in its publication *RV Ratings Guide* (CD-ROM) by highway control, reliability and value. This guide is designed as a research tool to help you make selections in motor homes, travel trailers, fifth wheels, slide-in campers, or fold-down tent trailers.

> ## To order call
> ## 1-800-405-3325
> ## or visit our website at
> ## rv.org

Other publications by JD Gallant:

The Green Book—RVs Rated
The Language of RVing
How to Buy an RV Without Getting Ripped Off
They're All Crooks!
How to Outwit Any Auto, Truck, or RV Dealer Every Time
How to Tow Safely CD

Coauthor:

The RV Ratings Guide CD
The RV Rating Book

About the Author

JD Gallant has been an RV enthusiast and RV trekker for over 35 years. He has authored several consumer books and has designed the database currently used by RV Consumer Group for rating recreational vehicles. In his professional life JD has been a technical writer, seminar speaker, school teacher, RV salesperson and advisor, quality control plant manager, and owner of automobile repair shops. Through his books, seminars, and workshops, he guides thousands of RVers on the right path to searching, selecting, buying, and enjoying their motor homes, travel trailers, and campers.

JD is one of the founders of RV Consumer Group, a nonprofit consumer organization dedicated to the safety of recreational vehicles. He serves on the Factory Assembled Structures Board in Washington State as an advocate of RV consumer programs emphasizing safety. He lives in Washington State.

Happy RVing!